The Complete XXL Air Fryer Cookbook UK

Affordable, Mouthwatering and Super-Delicious Air Fryer Recipes for Everyday Enjoyment I incl. Sides, Lunch, Breakfast & More I Collection of Family Favourites

Simon Brookfield

Copyright © [2023] [Simon Brookfield]

All rights reserved

All rights for this book here presented belong exclusively to the author. Usage or reproduction of the text is forbidden and requires a clear consent of the author in case of expectations.

ISBN - 9798373507691

Table of Contents

What is an Air Fryer? 8
What is the Difference Between an Air Fryer and a Deep Fryer? 9
What Can You Cook in an Air Fryer? 9
How Do Air Fryers Work? 10
Who Can Use an Air Fryer? 11
How Do You Use an Air Fryer? 11
What is the Best Air Fryer to Use? 12
What Are the Advantages of Using an Air Fryer? 13
    No Preheating is Required 13
    They Are Fast and Efficient at Cooking Your Food 13
    You Don't Need to Add Lots of Oil 14
    They Are Quick and Easy to Clean 14
    You Can Use Them to Cook a Large Variety of Different Foods 15
    They Take Up Very Little Space in Your Kitchen 15
What Are the Disadvantages of Using an Air Fryer? 15
    Breakfast 18
        Air Fryer Apple and Cinnamon Fritters 19
        Spinach and Egg Air Fryer Breakfast Cups 21
        Air Fryer Breakfast Burritos 22
        Air Fryer Cinnamon Rolls 24
        Air Fryer English Breakfast 26
        Air Fryer Cheesy Rolls 27
        Two Ingredient Air Fryer Banana Pancakes 29
        Air Fryer French Toast 30
        Fruity Air Fryer Pop Tarts 31

The Complete XXL Air Fryer Cookbook UK

Lunch 33
Air Fryer Turkey Burgers 34
Air Fryer Lemon Cod 35
Air Fryer Chicken Wings 36
Sticky Air Fryer Tofu 37
Air Fryer Crab Cakes with Tartar Sauce 39
Air Fryer Falafel with Tahini Sauce 41
Air Fryer Salmon Patties 43
Air Fryer Ham and Egg Pastry Pockets 44

Lunchtime Favourites 45
Air Fryer Chicken Parmesan 46
Air Fryer Cod With Lemon and Dill 48
Garlic Butter Air Fryer Steak 49
Air Fryer Roast Pork 51
Air Fryer Naan Pizzas 52
Air Fryer Sausage Biscuits 53
Air Fryer Lemon Shrimp 55
Air Fryer Fried Chicken 56
Southern Style Air Fryer Chicken 57
Sweet and Sticky Air Fryer Meatballs 58

Sides 60
Air Fryer Garlic Bread 61
Crispy Air Fryer Chickpeas 62
Air Fryer Potatoes 63
Air Fryer Sweet Potato Fries 64
Air Fryer Mixed Vegetables 65
Air Fryer Broccoli 66
Air Fryer Buffalo Cauliflower with Blue Cheese Sauce 67
Air Fryer Honey Carrots 69
Air Fryer Fried Rice 70
Crispy Cinnamon French Toast 71
Air Fryer Eggy Bread 72
Egg Fried Rice 73
Cauliflower with Hot Sauce and Blue Cheese Sauce 74
Sweet Potato Wedges 76

- Homemade Croquettes...77
- Sweet and Sticky Parsnips and Carrots 78
- BBQ Beetroot Crisps 79
- Cheesy Broccoli..80

Beef and Pork 81
- Sausage Burritos..82
- Crispy Chili Sausages 84
- Beef Stroganoff..85
- Beef Satay 86
- Homemade Crispy Pepperoni Pizza..87
- Pulled Pork, Bacon, and Cheese Sliders..89
- Sweet and Sticky Ribs..90

Poultry and Fish 92
- Air Fryer BBQ and Cheddar Chicken..93
- Air Fryer Chicken Wings..95
- Southern Fried Crispy Air Fryer Chicken 96
- Air Fryer BBQ Chicken..97
- Turkey Meatballs 98
- Air Fryer Tuna and Sweetcorn Sandwiches..99
- Crispy Salmon 100
- Tuna Patties..101
- Sticky Soy Sauce and Ginger Glazed Cod..102

Vegetarian and Vegan 103
- Roasted Vegetable Pasta..104
- Spinach and Egg Air Fryer Breakfast Muffins..105
- Vegan Meatballs...106
- Spring Ratatouille..108
- Sticky Tofu With Cauliflower Rice..109
- Chickpea and Sweetcorn Falafel 111
- Air Fryer Cheese Sandwich 113
- Spinach and Feta Croissants...114
- Tomato and Herb Tofu 115

The Complete XXL Air Fryer Cookbook UK

Desserts and Snacks — 117
- Air Fryer Oatmeal and Chocolate Chip Cookies — 118
- Air Fryer Banana Bread — 120
- Air Fryer Nutella Wedges — 122
- Air Fryer Chocolate Peanut Butter Cake — 123
- Air Fryer Puff Pastry Cherry Pies — 125
- Air Fryer Chocolate Donuts — 127
- Air Fryer Biscuits — 129
- Air Fryer Chocolate Brownies — 130
- Air Fryer Lava Cake — 131
- Chocolate and Berry Pop Tarts — 133
- White Chocolate Pudding — 135
- Milk and White Chocolate Chip Air Fryer Donuts with Frosting — 136
- Coffee, Chocolate Chip, and Banana Bread — 139
- White Chocolate and Raspberry Loaf — 141
- Chocolate-Glazed Banana Slices — 143
- Chocolate Souffle — 144
- Apple and Cinnamon Puff Pastry Pies — 145

Disclaimer — 148

EXCLUSIVE BONUS

40 Weight Loss Recipes

&

14 Days Meal Plan

Scan the QR-Code and receive the FREE download:

What is an Air Fryer?

An air fryer is used in the same way that an oven is used in the kitchen. People cook and roast different ingredients using specialised heating elements that sit at the top of the machine. Alongside these heating elements, there is a large fan that promotes faster convection and more efficient cooking. This results in deliciously crispy and fresh food.

The air fryer was patented by Philips Electronic Company a while back. The patent describes the kitchen appliance that is used as a healthier alternative to deep frying by using hot air and little or no oil.

The main reason why people choose to use an air fryer over other methods of cooking is that they require a lot less oil than deep frying.

They're also much quicker at cooking lots of food than an oven due to the close proximity of the heating elements to the ingredients that are being cooked and the powerful fan aiding the cooking process. You can get a healthier meal in a shorter amount of time, and that's enough to make anybody fall in love with the amazing air fryer.

We will talk more about the many benefits of using an air fryer over other cooking techniques further on in this book. First, we will quickly cover the key differences between the air fryer and the deep fryer because many people get confused between the two.

What is the Difference Between an Air Fryer and a Deep Fryer?

Unlike deep fryers that cook your food in a large amount of hot oil, air fryers do not require anywhere near as much oil. Instead, they use heating elements and a large fan to bake the ingredients until they are fully cooked.

Deep fryers heat the oil up to a certain temperature to cook your food quickly and easily. Therefore, you have to wait for the machine to heat up before you can begin adding your ingredients and this can add a significant amount of time to your cooking process.

Air fryers don't require any time to preheat before you can start cooking. You can add your ingredients and get started immediately. Plus, you won't need to add oil to your air fryer. Because of this, your food won't necessarily be fried. It will be baked.

If you use an air fryer, you also won't get the same batter coating that can be achieved when you use a deep fryer. If you do want to use a batter and cook it using an air fryer, you'll need to spray cooking oil over the food before placing it into the machine. This oil will enable the food to absorb the oil and form a delicious, crispy batter.

What Can You Cook in an Air Fryer?

As you will see as you read through this book, you will notice the huge variety of different meals and snacks that you can cook using an air fryer. Whether you want to cook fresh meats, fish, and vegetables or you need to defrost and cook frozen foods, you can do all of this in your trusted air fryer.

Most meats will require a little more oil to be added so they can cook properly but it's still much less than the amount of oil you'd use in a deep fryer. If your meats are marinated in a lot of sauce, you might not need to add any oil but this will be specified in the recipe you're following.

Similarly, your veggies will also need a quick coating of oil if you want them to come out extra crispy.

It's recommended that you use vegetable oil instead of butter when cooking in an air fryer. This is because oil heats up much more quickly than butter due to its higher smoke point. It can also withstand the high temperatures of the air fryer. All of the recipes in this book will use olive oil but almost any plant-based oil should be fine to use in your machine.

How Do Air Fryers Work?

Air fryers work via a heating mechanism that sits near to the top of the machine and a large fan that may be placed lower down or along the sides of the machine. The inner compartment of the air fryer has a mesh basket and it's in here that you place your ingredients.

When you turn the air fryer on, the elements will immediately begin to heat up. The large fan will begin turning to circulate the hot air around the inner compartment. This rapid circulation will heat your food and leave it golden and crispy.

Who Can Use an Air Fryer?

The beauty of air fryers is that anybody can use them. They're simple and easy to operate, and they're an affordable kitchen gadget. They don't require very much space in your kitchen but they can provide you will a healthy method of cooking so you can create whatever recipes you like.

Maybe you're brand-new to cooking and you're looking for an easy way to bring your favourite recipes into life. Or maybe you're a professional chef that wants an efficient way to cook complex meals at home. Or maybe you're somewhere in between the two and you class yourself as an average cook.

Whatever part of the cooking spectrum you fall on, an air fryer will be appropriate for you! Even if you're a little uncertain how to properly operate your air fryer at first, you'll get more comfortable using the machine over time. Before you know it, you'll be cooking delicious dishes with ease.

How Do You Use an Air Fryer?

Most air fryers will come with an instruction manual for you to refer to when you're cooking but here are some general guidelines to help you out.

1. Place your ingredients into the mesh basket inside the air fryer. Depending on the size of your air fryer, you'll need to adjust the amount of food you use. Be careful not to overfill the air fryer as this might affect the cooking process.
2. Add extra oil if you're using any. Toss the ingredients around to coat them in the oil.

3. Set the time and temperature. Most air fryers have pre-set times and temperatures that make it really simple to cook your ingredients for the right amount of time. Usually, times range from 5 to 30 minutes and temperature settings are between 180 and 250 degrees Celsius.
4. Sit back and allow the air fryer to do its thing. Once you've prepped your food and set your time and temperature, you can leave the air fryer to cook your ingredients.
5. Once your food is ready, leave the air fryer to cool down before you wipe it clean.

What is the Best Air Fryer to Use?

There are several different air fryers available on the market. They all have different features and settings, so the one that is right for you will depend on your needs and preferences.

However, we've compiled a quick list of some of the best options if you have no idea which one to buy.

- ★ Philips Avance Turbo-Star Air Fryer
- ★ NINJA Foodi MAX 14-in-1 SmartLid Air Fryer
- ★ Black and Decker Purify Air Fryer
- ★ Tower T17023 Air Fryer
- ★ PowerXL Vortex Air Fryer
- ★ COSORI Air Fryer Air Fryer

Take a look at each option and determine which one suits your needs the best. Remember to take into account the price of each one as the cost can vary significantly from brand to brand.

What Are the Advantages of Using an Air Fryer?

There are lots of advantages to owning an air fryer and using it to cook your meals and snacks. Here are some of the main benefits.

No Preheating is Required

When you're using an air fryer, you don't need to wait for the elements to preheat and you won't need to wait for large volumes of oil to get hot before you add your ingredients either (because you don't really need any oil)!

Due to the lack of preheating, your cooking process will be much quicker and easier. If you're looking for a way to streamline your cooking process and reduce the time you spend in the kitchen, an air fryer might just be the perfect option for you.

They Are Fast and Efficient at Cooking Your Food

Because of the hot heating elements and the large fan that is able to circulate the hot air inside the cooking basket, air fryers are extremely efficient at cooking your food. They also cook your food nice and evenly, so you can rest assured knowing that all of your meat and fish ingredients are fully cooked all the way through.

The speedy cooking process creates a delicious, crispy coating over your food, which is something that you'll only get with the amazing air fryer!

You Don't Need to Add Lots of Oil

Many people love the crispy coating that they get on their food when they use a deep fryer. But unfortunately, deep fryers require a lot of oil to be added so that your food can be cooked properly.

With an air fryer, you don't need to add any oil at all with most ingredients and you only need to add a tiny bit when you're using meats and vegetables. This makes your resulting dish healthier and less oily, but just as delicious.

If you're trying to cut back on your saturated fat intake or reduce your calories to lose weight, switching your usual deep fryer for an air fryer will help you along your weight loss journey.

They Are Quick and Easy to Clean

Most air fryers have pre-made settings that make it easy for you to select a cooking time and temperature. All you need to do is add your ingredients and select the right setting for your needs.

This makes air fryers easy to use for everybody, even those who have never set foot in the kitchen before. It also makes these handy kitchen gadgets much quicker to operate and organise when you're in the middle of the cooking process.

As soon as your food is cooked, you can quickly wipe down the outside of the machine with a cloth and spray. Once the machine has cooled down, you can use the same cloth to give the inner component a good clean. The mesh basket is removable and is dish washer friendly too.

You Can Use Them to Cook a Large Variety of Different Foods

This recipe book is just a dip in the water when it comes to the vast array of different air fryer recipes that are available for you to follow. Whether you're looking for some exciting breakfast recipes, lunchtime creations, or evening meals to create, there is no shortage of air fryer friendly recipes for you to browse online or in cookbooks like this one.

For those of you who love variety in your meals, you won't be disappointed with the range of different dishes that the air fryer can be used to produce. Each night will present the opportunity for a brand-new exciting meal for you to try.

They Take Up Very Little Space in Your Kitchen

Air fryers are neat and compact. They take up very little room in your kitchen, making them ideal for people who have smaller cooking areas. They're suitable for storing in your cupboards as well because they're portable and lightweight.

Most of them come in a sleek black or silver colour, so they look great when left out on your kitchen countertop. And since they're very compact, they won't get in your way while you're trying to cook.

What Are the Disadvantages of Using an Air Fryer?

It's only fair that we mention some of the potential disadvantages to using an air fryer. Although, we strongly believe that the advantages far outweigh the drawbacks!

The two main disadvantages of using an air fryer are:

- There is an increased risk of your food burning due to the rapid heating of the elements in the machine.
- Because no oil is used, you might miss out on healthy monounsaturated and polyunsaturated fats. Of course, you can get your fats from elsewhere in your diet but plant-based oils are one of the best ways to increase your intake of omega-3 and omega-6 fatty acids.

To get around these problems, keep an eye on your food when it's cooking in the air fryer. If it looks like it's about to burn, turn the temperature down ever so slightly.

If you want to increase your healthy fat intake, you could add a tiny splash of oil into your air fryer. Alternatively, you can increase your intake of the following foods, all of which contain lots of unsaturated fats:

- Avocados
- Nuts and seeds
- Fatty fish
- Pulses and legumes
- Beans

EXCLUSIVE BONUS

40 Weight Loss Recipes

&

14 Days Meal Plan

Scan the QR-Code and receive the FREE download:

BREAKFAST

Simon Brookfield

Air Fryer Apple and Cinnamon Fritters

Makes 4 servings
Preparation time – 20 minutes
Cooking time – 5 minutes
Nutritional values per serving – 102 kcals, 17 g carbs, 4 g protein, 4 g fat

Ingredients

- 2 green apples
- 200 g / 7 oz plain flour
- 2 tbsp brown sugar
- 1 tsp baking powder
- ½ tsp salt
- 1 tsp ground cinnamon
- 1 tsp ground nutmeg
- 2 tbsp butter
- 1 egg
- 100 ml milk

Method

1. Peel the apples and cut them into small chunks. Set aside in a bowl.
2. In a large mixing bowl, mix the plain flour, brown sugar, baking powder, salt, ground cinnamon, and ground nutmeg together until combined.
3. Place the butter in a heatproof bowl and heat in the microwave for 30 seconds until melted.
4. Crack the egg into the butter and mix to combine. Stir in the milk and mix well.
5. Fold the wet mixture into the dry mixture until fully incorporated into a soft dough.
6. Cover the bowl of dough with tin foil and place in the fridge to cool for 10 minutes.
7. Meanwhile, preheat the air fryer to 180 °C / 350 °F and line the bottom of the basket with parchment paper.
8. Remove the dough from the fridge and use a spoon to create small fritters. Place the fritters into the air fryer and cook for 5-6 minutes until crispy.

Spinach and Egg Air Fryer Breakfast Cups

Makes 4 servings
Preparation time – 5 minutes
Cooking time – 10 minutes
Nutritional values per serving – 176 kcals, 10 g carbs, 8 g protein, 7 g fat

Ingredients

- 8 eggs
- 100 g / 3.5 oz fresh spinach
- 50 g / 1.8 oz cheddar cheese, grated
- 1 tsp black pepper

Method

1. Preheat your air fryer to 200 °C / 400 °F and line an 8-pan muffin tray with parchment paper or grease with olive oil.
2. Gently press the spinach leaves into the bottom of each prepared muffin cup.
3. Crack 2 eggs into each cup on top of the spinach and top each with grated cheddar cheese and a sprinkle of black pepper.
4. Place the muffins into the air fryer, close the lid, and cook for 10 minutes until the eggs are set.
5. Serve while hot for breakfast.

Air Fryer Breakfast Burritos

Makes 4 servings
Preparation time – 20 minutes
Cooking time – 20 minutes
Nutritional values per serving – 450 kcals, 31 g carbs, 10 g protein, 12 g fat

Ingredients

- 1 medium white potato
- 2 tbsp olive oil
- 1 tsp salt
- 1 tsp black pepper
- 8 raw sausages
- 4 wholemeal flour tortillas
- 4 eggs
- 200 ml milk
- 100 g / 3.5 oz cheddar cheese, grated

Method

1. Preheat your air fryer to 200 °C / 400 °F and line the bottom of the basket with parchment paper.
2. Peel the potato and cut into small cubes. Place in a bowl and toss in 1 tbsp olive oil, and a pinch of salt and pepper.
3. Place the potato cubes into the air fryer and cook for 7-8 minutes. Remove and set aside on paper towels to drain.
4. Heat 1 tbsp olive oil in a medium skillet and add the sausages. Cook for 5 minutes until slightly browned. Remove the sausages and set aside. Leave the sausage juices in the pan.
5. In a bowl, whisk the eggs and milk, and pour into the hot skillet. Cook the eggs, using a fork or spoon to scramble them. Remove from the skillet and set aside.
6. In a large bowl, mix together the potatoes, sausages, scrambled eggs, and cheddar cheese.
7. Spread the mixture evenly across the 4 wholemeal flour tortillas and roll up into burritos. Use a toothpick to keep them together.
8. Place the burritos into the hot air fryer and cook for 7-8 minutes, turning halfway through.
9. Enjoy for breakfast with a hot cup of coffee or tea.

Air Fryer Cinnamon Rolls

Makes 8 servings
Preparation time – 10 minutes
Cooking time – 10 minutes
Nutritional values per serving – 299 kcals, 19 g carbs, 3 g protein, 18 g fat

Ingredients

For the cinnamon rolls:

- 1 tbsp ground cinnamon
- 100 g / 3.5 oz butter
- 6 tbsp brown sugar
- 1 sheet frozen puff pastry, thawed

For the Icing:

- 50 g / 1.8 oz icing sugar
- 2 tbsp milk

Method

1. Preheat your air fryer to 200 °C / 400 °F and line the bottom of the basket with parchment paper.
2. In a small mixing bowl, combine the cinnamon, butter, and brown sugar.
3. Roll out the puff pastry sheet and spread the cinnamon mixture evenly across the whole sheet.
4. Roll the puff pastry into swirls and cut into 2-inch pieces.
5. Transfer the cinnamon roll pieces into the preheated air fryer and cook for 7-8 minutes until golden and crispy.
6. While the cinnamon rolls are cooking, combine the icing sugar and milk to form a thick icing. Add a little bit of water if the mixture looks too dry and crumbly.
7. When the cinnamon rolls are cooked, spread the icing sugar evenly over the top of the rolls. Leave the set and enjoy while warm.

Air Fryer English Breakfast

Makes 2 servings
Preparation time – 5 minutes
Cooking time – 15 minutes
Nutritional values per serving – 315 kcals, 18 g carbs, 6 g protein, 12 g fat

Ingredients

- 2 eggs, beaten
- 2 tbsp milk
- 1 tbsp butter
- 1 tsp salt
- 1 tsp black pepper
- 6 sausages
- 6 bacon rashers
- 4 small black pudding
- 4 large tomatoes
- 1 x 400 g / 14 oz can baked beans

Method

1. Preheat your air fryer to 180 °C / 350 °F and line the bottom of the basket with parchment paper.
2. In a bowl, whisk together the eggs, milk, butter, salt, and black pepper. Pour the mixture into the air fryer.
3. Add the sausages, bacon rashers, black pudding, and tomatoes. Close the lid of the air fryer and cook for 10 minutes.
4. After 10 minutes, the egg should be cooked. Remove the eggs from the air fryer and add the baked beans in their place.
5. Cook for 5 further minutes.
6. Serve the breakfast with an extra sprinkle of black pepper.

Simon Brookfield

Air Fryer Cheesy Rolls

Makes 8 servings
Preparation time – 30 minutes
Cooking time – 10 minutes
Nutritional values per serving – 278 kcals, 16 g carbs, 8 g protein, 15 g fat

Ingredients

- 1 tbsp olive oil
- 8 sausages
- ½ onion, sliced
- 100 g / 3.5 g cheddar cheese, grated
- 100 g / 3.5 g Parmesan cheese, grated
- 4 eggs, beaten
- 1 tbsp butter
- 1 tbsp milk
- 1 tsp salt
- ½ tsp black pepper
- 12 egg roll wrappers

Method

1. Preheat your air fryer to 180 °C / 350 °F and line the bottom of the basket with parchment paper.
2. In a small skillet, heat 1 tbsp olive oil and cook the sausages and onion slices for 4-5 minutes. Set aside.
3. In a bowl, mix the cheddar cheese and Parmesan cheese with the eggs, butter, milk, salt, and black pepper until combined.
4. Cut the sausages into small slices and add to the cheese mixture along with the onions.
5. Spread the ingredients evenly into each egg roll wrapper and fold tightly. Use cocktail sticks to keep them closed if necessary.
6. Add the rolls to the air fryer, close the lid, and cook for 3-4 minutes until golden and crispy.
7. Serve hot with some salsa or a drizzle of maple syrup.

Two Ingredient Air Fryer Banana Pancakes

Makes 2 servings
Preparation time – 5 minutes
Cooking time – 10 minutes
Nutritional values per serving – 135 kcals, 6 g carbs, 4 g protein, 5 g fat

Ingredients

- 2 bananas
- 2 eggs, beaten

Method

1. Preheat your air fryer to 180 °C / 350 °F and line the bottom of the basket with parchment paper.
2. Peel the bananas and mash in a bowl using a fork.
3. Whisk in the eggs until combined.
4. Pour half of the batter into the hot air fryer and allow it to spread into a pancake shape across the bottom of the machine.
5. Cook for 10 minutes until golden and crispy.
6. Carefully remove the pancake and set aside. Repeat steps 4 and 5 with the remaining half of the batter.
7. Serve the pancakes hot with some maple syrup, extra banana slices, and strawberry slices, or any other toppings of your choice.

Air Fryer French Toast

Makes 2 servings
Preparation time – 10 minutes
Cooking time – 5 minutes
Nutritional values per serving – 256 kcals, 16 g carbs, 5 g protein, 5 g fat

Ingredients

- 4 slices bread
- 4 eggs
- 200 ml milk
- 2 tbsp sugar
- 1 tsp vanilla extract
- ½ tsp ground cinnamon
- 1 tbsp maple syrup

Method

1. Preheat your air fryer to 150 °C / 300 °F and line the bottom of the basket with parchment paper.
2. Cut the bread into 2 even rectangles. Set aside.
3. In a mixing bowl, whisk together the 4 eggs, milk, sugar, vanilla extract, and ground cinnamon.
4. Soak the bread pieces in the egg mixture so that they are fully covered. They should take around 2 minutes.
5. Place the soaked bread slices in the lined air fryer baskets, close the lid, and cook for 4-5 minutes.
6. Serve the French toast slices with a drizzle of maple syrup and a sprinkle of extra sugar if desired.

Simon Brookfield

Fruity Air Fryer Pop Tarts

Makes 8 servings
Preparation time – 15 minutes
Cooking time – 10 minutes
Nutritional values per serving – 234 kcals, 28 g carbs, 3 g protein, 12 g fat

Ingredients

For the filling:

- 100 g / 3.5 oz fresh blueberries
- 50 g / 1.8 oz fresh raspberries
- 50 g / 1.8 oz fresh strawberries
- 100 g / 3.5 oz sugar
- 1 tsp corn starch

For the pastry:

- 1 sheet puff pastry
- For the frosting:
- 4 tbsp powdered sugar
- 2 tbsp maple syrup from the berry compote
- 1 tbsp lemon juice

Method

1. Preheat your air fryer to 180 °C / 350 °F and line the bottom of the basket with parchment paper.
2. Begin making the filling by placing the blueberries, strawberries, raspberries, and sugar in a large saucepan over a medium heat. Bring the mixture to a boil while stirring and breaking the berries up.
3. Stir in the corn starch and allow the mixture to simmer for 1-2 minutes. Remove the pan from the heat and set aside.
4. To make the pastry, roll out the sheet of puff pastry and cut it into 8 equal rectangles.
5. Spoon 2 tbsp of the berry filling onto one side of each rectangle. Fold the other side of each puff pastry rectangle over to cover the filling. Use a fork to seal the edges.
6. Transfer the filled puff pastry rectangles to the prepared air fryer basket. Close the lid and cook for 10 minutes until the pastry is golden and crispy. Remove from the air fryer and set aside to cool.
7. While the puff pastry rectangles are cooling, make the frosting by combining the powdered sugar, maple syrup, and lemon juice in a bowl. Whisk well until it forms a smooth mixture.
8. Drizzle the frosting over the top of the cooled pop tarts and enjoy!

LUNCH

Air Fryer Turkey Burgers

Makes 4 servings
Preparation time – 5 minutes
Cooking time – 15 minutes
Nutritional values per serving – 310 kcals, 14 g carbs, 21 g protein, 10 g fat

Ingredients

- 400 g / 14 oz ground turkey
- 1 tsp cajun seasoning
- 1 tsp ground cumin
- 1 tsp onion powder
- 1 tsp garlic powder
- 2 tbsp dried mixed herbs
- ½ tsp salt
- ½ tsp black pepper
- 1 egg, beaten
- 1 tbsp soy sauce

Method

1. Preheat your air fryer to 200 °C / 400 °F and line the bottom of the basket with parchment paper.
2. In a mixing bowl, combine the ground turkey, cajun seasoning, onion powder, garlic powder, dried mixed herbs, salt, and black pepper in a bowl. Mix until combined.
3. Add the egg and soy sauce and mix well until all of the ingredients are fully incorporated.
4. Shape the mixture into 4 even patties. Transfer the patties into the prepared air fryer basket and cook for 15-20 minutes, turning halfway through, until fully cooked. The burgers should be golden and crispy.
5. Serve the burgers in a burger bun with some added salad and your favourite sauce.

Air Fryer Lemon Cod

Makes 4 servings
Preparation time – 5 minutes
Cooking time – 10 minutes
Nutritional values per serving – 185 kcals, 4 g carbs, 19 g protein, 6 g fat

Ingredients

- 4 x 100 g / 3.5 oz cod fillets
- 3 tbsp unsalted butter, melted
- 1 lemon, halved
- ½ tsp salt
- ½ tsp black pepper

Method

1. Preheat your air fryer to 200 °C / 400 °F and line the bottom of the basket with parchment paper.
2. Place the cod fillets on a clean surface. Use a pastry brush to coat the top of the fillets with melted butter.
3. Squeeze the juice of one half of the lemon over the top of each buttered cod fillet and add a sprinkle a pinch of salt and black pepper onto each.
4. Cut the other half of the lemon into slices and add one slice onto each cod fillet.
5. Transfer the fillets to the air fryer, close the lid, and cook for 10 minutes until the fish is tender and falls apart with a fork.
6. Eat the fish while still hot with a side of new potatoes and vegetables.

Air Fryer Chicken Wings

Makes 4 servings
Preparation time – 10 minutes
Cooking time – 20 minutes
Nutritional values per serving – 99 kcals, 6 g carbs, 2 g protein, 6 g fat

Ingredients

- 400 g / 14 oz chicken wings
- 1 tsp salt
- 1 tsp black pepper
- 4 tbsp hot sauce
- 4 tbsp olive oil
- 1 tbsp soy sauce
- 1 tsp garlic powder

Method

1. Preheat your air fryer to 200 °C / 400 °F and line the bottom of the basket with parchment paper.
2. Season the wings with salt and pepper. Place them in the air fryer, close the lid of the machine, and cook for 12-15 minutes.
3. Meanwhile, add the hot sauce, olive oil, soy sauce, and garlic powder to a bowl. Whisk together into a sauce.
4. Remove the chicken wings from the air fryer and toss in the hot sauce mixture until every wing is fully coated.
5. Return the wings to the air fryer and cook for a further 5 minutes.
6. Serve the wings while still piping hot.

Sticky Air Fryer Tofu

Makes 4 servings
Preparation time – 30 minutes
Cooking time – 15 minutes
Nutritional values per serving – 299 kcals, 8 g carbs, 13 g protein, 5 g fat

Ingredients

- 1 tsp onion powder
- 1 tsp garlic powder
- 1 tsp smoked paprika
- 2 tbsp soy sauce
- 2 tbsp sweet chili sauce
- 2 tbsp sriracha
- 1 x 400 g / 14 oz block firm tofu, cubed
- 3 tbsp corn starch
- 1 tsp black pepper

Method

1. Preheat your air fryer to 150 °C / 300 °F and line the bottom of the basket with parchment paper.
2. In a small mixing bowl, add the onion powder, garlic powder, smoked paprika, soy sauce, sweet chili sauce, and sriracha. Mix well.
3. Toss the tofu cubes in the sauce to fully coat on all sides. Place in the fridge for 20 minutes to marinate.
4. In a bowl, whisk together the corn starch and pepper. Coat the tofu in the corn starch mixture and add to the lined air fryer basket.
5. Close the lid of the machine and cook the tofu cubes for 15 minutes until golden and crispy.
6. Serve hot with an extra drizzle of sweet chili sauce and a side of noodles and veggies.

Air Fryer Crab Cakes with Tartar Sauce

Makes 4 servings
Preparation time – 20 minutes
Cooking time – 15 minutes
Nutritional values per serving – 243 kcals, 11 g carbs, 13 g protein, 8 g fat

Ingredients

For the crab cakes:

- 3 tbsp mayonnaise
- 1 egg
- 2 tbsp dried mixed herbs
- 2 tsp Dijon mustard
- 1 tsp lemon zest
- 1 tbs salt
- 400 g / 14 oz crab meat
- 8 wholemeal crackers, crushed

For the Tartar sauce:

- 4 tbsp mayonnaise
- ½ shallot, finely chopped
- 2 tsp capers, finely chopped
- 1 tsp lemon juice
- ½ tsp Dijon mustard
- 1 tsp fresh dill, finely chopped

Method

1. For the crab cakes, whisk together the mayonnaise, egg, dried mixed herbs, Dijon mustard, lemon zest, and salt.
2. Fold in the crab meat and wholemeal crackers until it is fully coated in the sauce.
3. Divide the mixture into 8 even patties and place them in the fridge for 15 minutes.
4. Preheat your air fryer to 200 °C / 400 °F and line the bottom of the basket with parchment paper.
5. Remove the crab cakes out of the fridge and place them in the lined air fryer basket. Cook the patties for 15 minutes, flipping halfway through.
6. Meanwhile, make the tartar sauce by combining all of the ingredients in a small mixing bowl.
7. Serve the crab cakes warm with tartar sauce and a side of your choice.

Air Fryer Falafel with Tahini Sauce

Makes 4 servings
Preparation time – 10 minutes
Cooking time – 15 minutes
Nutritional values per serving – 178 kcals, 12 g carbs, 10 g protein, 9 g fat

Ingredients

For the falafel:

- ½ onion, sliced
- 4 cloves garlic, peeled and sliced
- 2 tbsp fresh parsley leaves, chopped
- 2 tbsp fresh coriander leaves, chopped
- 2 x 400 g / 14 oz chickpeas, drained and rinsed
- 1 tsp salt
- 1 tsp baking powder
- 1 tsp dried mixed herbs
- ½ tsp crushed red pepper flakes

For the tahini sauce:

- 3 tbsp tahini
- Juice ½ lemon
- 3 tbsp water, plus more if needed

Method

1. Preheat your air fryer to 180 °C / 350 °F and line the bottom of the basket with parchment paper.
2. Place the onion, garlic cloves, fresh parsley, and fresh coriander in a food processor. Pulse in 30-second intervals until fully combined, scraping the mixture from the sides of the food processor in between each interval if necessary.
3. Add the chickpeas, salt, baking powder, dried mixed herbs, and crushed red pepper flakes. Pulse the mixture until fully combined. Add more water if necessary. The mixture should be dry but not crumbly. It should form more of a paste-like texture.
4. Scoop out about 2 tbsp of the mixture at a time and roll into small balls. Place the falafel balls into the prepared air fryer basket and cook for 15 minutes.
5. While the falafels are cooking, make the tahini sauce by combining all of the ingredients in a bowl.
6. Serve the falafels hot or cold with a drizzle of tahini sauce. To make the meal more substantial, serve in wholemeal pitta bread with some salad.

Air Fryer Salmon Patties

Makes 4 servings
Preparation time – 15 minutes
Cooking time – 10 minutes
Nutritional values per serving – 276 kcals, 10 g carbs, 18 g protein, 15 g fat

Ingredients

- 1 x 400 g / 14 oz canned salmon, drained and mashed
- 2 eggs
- 4 tbsp mayonnaise
- 1 tsp salt
- 100 g / 3.5 oz breadcrumbs
- 2 tbsp plain yoghurt
- Juice 1 lemon

Method

1. Preheat your air fryer to 180 °C / 350 °F and line the bottom of the basket with parchment paper.
2. In a large mixing bowl, combine the salmon, eggs, mayonnaise, salt, breadcrumbs, yoghurt, and juice of 1 lemon.
3. Scoop small batches of the mixture out of the bowl and shape into patties using your hands. Make sure the patties are no thicker than 1 inch and try to make each patty the same thickness.
4. Place the patties in the air fryer and cook for 10 minutes, turning halfway through. The patties should be golden and crispy.
5. Serve with a side salad and some extra yoghurt to dip your patties into.

Air Fryer Ham and Egg Pastry Pockets

Makes 2 servings
Preparation time – 15 minutes
Cooking time – 15 minutes
Nutritional values per serving – 335 kcals, 23 g carbs, 10 g protein, 18 g fat

Ingredients

- 1 egg
- 2 tbsp milk
- 2 tbsp butter
- 400 g / 14 oz ham, diced
- 50 g / 3.5 oz cheddar cheese, grated
- 2 crescent rolls

Method

1. Preheat your air fryer to 180 °C / 350 °F and line the bottom of the basket with parchment paper.
2. In a small bowl, combine 1 egg and 2 tbsp milk.
3. Heat the 2 tbsp butter in a skillet and add the egg mixture. Cook for 5 minutes until the eggs are set and scrambled.
4. Remove the eggs from the heat and place in a bowl. Fold in the ham and cheddar cheese.
5. Spoon half of the filling into each crescent roll. Fold the rolls over to cover the filling and pinch the edges to seal.
6. Place the filled crescent rolls basket, close the lid, and cook for 8-10 minutes until golden brown and slightly crispy on the edges.

Simon Brookfield

LUNCHTIME FAVOURITES

Air Fryer Chicken Parmesan

Makes 4 servings
Preparation time – 15 minutes
Cooking time – 10 minutes
Nutritional values per serving – 297 kcals, 13 g carbs, 14 g protein, 11 g fat

Ingredients

- 400 g / 14 oz skinless, boneless chicken breasts
- 1 tsp salt
- 1 tsp black pepper
- 50 g / 1.8 oz Parmesan cheese, grated
- 100 g / 3.5 oz plain flour
- 2 eggs
- 100 g / 3.5 oz panko breadcrumbs
- ½ tsp garlic powder
- ½ tsp onion powder
- ½ tsp dried oregano
- 8 tbsp marinara sauce
- 100 g / 3.5 oz cheddar cheese, grated

Simon Brookfield

Method

1. Preheat your air fryer to 200 °C / 400 °F and line the bottom of the basket with parchment paper.
2. Cut the chicken breasts in half and season with salt and pepper.
3. Place the Parmesan cheese in a small bowl and add the garlic powder, onion powder, and dried oregano. Stuff the Parmesan cheese mixture into each chicken breast and press the edges down to seal the mixture inside the breasts.
4. Place the flour in a small mixing bowl, crack the eggs into a separate bowl and whisk well, and place the panko breadcrumbs into a third bowl.
5. Coat the chicken breasts in the flour, followed by the egg mixture, followed by the panko breadcrumbs. By the end, the chicken breasts should be fully coated in the breadcrumbs.
6. Place the chicken breasts into the lined air fryer basket and cook for 5 minutes. Add the cheddar cheese on top of each chicken breast and continue cooking for a further 5 minutes until the chicken is crispy and golden and the cheese is melted.
7. Meanwhile, place the marinara sauce in a heat proof bowl and heat for 30-60 seconds until hot.
8. Serve the chicken with the hot marinara sauce on top.

Air Fryer Cod With Lemon and Dill

Makes 4 servings
Preparation time – 10 minutes
Cooking time – 10 minutes
Nutritional values per serving – 302 kcals, 5 g carbs, 30 g protein, 12 g fat

Ingredients

- 4 x 100 g / 3.5 oz cod fillets
- 4 tbsp butter, melted
- 6 garlic cloves, peeled and minced
- 2 tbsp lemon juice
- 2 tbsp fresh dill, finely chopped
- ½ tsp salt

Method

1. Preheat your air fryer to 180 °C / 350 °F and line the bottom of the basket with parchment paper.
2. Lay the cod fillets out on a clean surface.
3. In a mixing bowl, combine the butter, garlic cloves, lemon juice, fresh dill, and salt.
4. Spoon the garlic butter mixture onto the top of each cod fillet and gently press down so the filling doesn't fall off during the cooking process.
5. Transfer the cod fillets into the lined air fryer basket. Make sure they aren't overlapping with one another.
6. Close the air fryer lid and cook for 10 minutes until the fish is cooked. It should fall apart when you break it using a fork.
7. Enjoy the cod fillets while warm with a side of rice and vegetables.

Garlic Butter Air Fryer Steak

Makes 2 servings
Preparation time – 10 minutes
Cooking time – 15 minutes
Nutritional values per serving – 414 kcals, 9 g carbs, 15 g protein, 10 g fat

Ingredients

- 4 tbsp butter, softened
- 2 garlic cloves, peeled and minced
- 2 tsp fresh parsley, chopped
- 1 tsp fresh chives, chopped
- 1 tsp fresh thyme, chopped
- 1 tbsp dried oregano
- 800 g / 28 oz rib-eye steak
- 1 tsp salt
- 1 tsp black pepper

Method

1. Preheat your air fryer to 200 °C / 400 °F and line the bottom of the basket with parchment paper.
2. Combine the butter, minced garlic, parsley, chives, thyme, and oregano in a mixing bowl.
3. Take an egg brush and lightly coat the steak with the garlic butter mixture on both sides. Don't use all of the mixture as most of it will be used for the garlic butter.
4. Place the remaining garlic butter in the freezer to harden while the steaks cook.
5. Place the steak in the lined air fryer basket, close the lid of the machine, and cook for 15 minutes, turning halfway through.
6. Remove the steaks from the air fryer and place the slightly hardened garlic butter in the centre of each steak.
7. Serve with a side of chips and salad.

Air Fryer Roast Pork

Makes 4 servings
Preparation time – 20 minutes
Cooking time – 15 minutes
Nutritional values per serving – 456 kcals, 12 g carbs, 18 g protein, 9 g fat

Ingredients

- 1 large pork loin
- 1 tsp salt
- 1 tsp black pepper

Method

1. Score the pork loin with a sharp knife.
2. Pat the rind dry with a paper towel and rub the salt and black pepper into it.
3. Place the pork loin in the fridge for 20 minutes.
4. Preheat your air fryer to 200 °C / 400 °F and line the bottom of the basket with parchment paper.
5. Transfer the pork loin into the air fryer, skin side up, and cook for 15 minutes until golden and crispy.
6. Set aside to cool for 15 minutes before cutting into slices.

Air Fryer Naan Pizzas

Makes 2 servings
Preparation time – 5 minutes
Cooking time – 5 minutes
Nutritional values per serving – 298 kcals, 15 g carbs, 9 g protein, 8 g fat

Ingredients

- 2 plain naan breads
- 2 tbsp tomato pasta
- 50 g / 1.8 oz cheddar cheese, grated
- 1 tsp dried mixed herbs

Method

1. Preheat your air fryer to 190 °C / 375 °F and line the bottom of the basket with parchment paper.
2. Spread 1 tbsp tomato paste onto each naan bread.
3. Top with the cheddar cheese and a sprinkle of dried mixed herbs.
4. Place the naan bread pizzas in the lined air fryer basket, close the lid of the machine, and cook for 5 minutes until the naans are golden and crunchy, and the cheese is melted.

Air Fryer Sausage Biscuits

Makes 4 servings
Preparation time – 5 minutes
Cooking time – 20 minutes
Nutritional values per serving – 189 kcals, 5 g carbs, 7 g protein, 10 g fat

Ingredients

- 1 tbsp olive oil
- 400 g / 14 oz sausage meat
- 2 eggs
- ½ salt
- ½ black pepper
- 100 g / 3.5 oz cheddar cheese, grated
- 400 g / 14 oz flaky biscuits

Method

1. Heat the olive oil in a skillet and add the sausages. Cook for 8-10 minutes until browned. Set aside to drain on paper towels.
2. In a mixing bowl, whisk together the eggs, salt, and black pepper. Add to the hot skillet and cook for 4-5 minutes until the eggs are slightly cooked and scrambled. They won't be fully cooked at this point, but they will cook further in when placed in the air fryer.
3. Preheat your air fryer to 180 °C / 350 °F and line the bottom of the basket with parchment paper.
4. Lay out half of the flaky biscuits and add the grated cheddar cheese evenly across the top. Top with the sausage meat and egg mixture and spread out evenly.
5. Top with the remaining half of the flaky biscuits and pinch the edges to seal the filling side.
6. Transfer the filled biscuits to the lined air fryer basket, close the lid, and cook for 5 minutes until golden brown.
7. Enjoy the sausage biscuits while hot.

Air Fryer Lemon Shrimp

Makes 4 servings
Preparation time – 5 minutes
Cooking time – 10 minutes
Nutritional values per serving – 334 kcals, 3 g carbs, 16 g protein, 12 g fat

Ingredients

- 400 g / 14 oz raw shrimp, peeled and deveined
- 2 tbsp olive oil
- 2 tbsp lemon juice
- 1 tsp salt
- 1 tsp black pepper

Method

1. Preheat your air fryer to 200 °C / 400 °F and line the bottom of the basket with parchment paper.
2. Place the shrimp in a mixing bowl and add the olive oil, lemon juice, salt, and black pepper. Toss to fully coat the shrimp.
3. Transfer the shrimp to the prepared air fryer basket and cook for 7-8 minutes until the shells turn pink and the shrimp is slightly white, but still slightly opaque.
4. Remove the shrimp from the air fryer and serve with your favourite sides.

Air Fryer Fried Chicken

Makes 8 servings
Preparation time – 10 minutes
Cooking time – 20 minutes
Nutritional values per serving – 445 kcals, 23 g carbs, 25 g protein, 18 g fat

Ingredients

- 200 ml buttermilk
- 2 eggs
- 800 g / 28 oz bone-in chicken thighs
- 200 g / 7 oz plain flour
- 2 tsp paprika
- 1 tsp mild chili powder
- 2 tsp garlic powder
- 2 tsp onion powder
- 1 tsp salt
- 1 tsp black pepper

Method

1. Preheat your air fryer to 200 °C / 400 °F and line the bottom of the basket with parchment paper.
2. In a large mixing bowl, whisk the buttermilk and eggs together until well combined.
3. In a separate bowl, combine the plain flour, paprika, chili powder, garlic powder, onion powder, salt, and black pepper. Mix well.
4. Use tongs to dip the chicken into the wet mixture, followed by the dry mixture to fully coat each thigh in spices.
5. Transfer the chicken thighs to the prepared air fryer basket. Cook for 20 minutes until the chicken thighs are cooked and crispy.
6. Serve warm with your favourite sides.

Simon Brookfield

Southern Style Air Fryer Chicken

Makes 4 servings
Preparation time – 15 minutes
Cooking time – 15 minutes
Nutritional values per serving – 372 kcals, 17 g carbs, 21 g protein, 13 g fat

Ingredients

- 200 g / 7 oz crackers
- 1 tsp fresh parsley, finely chopped
- 1 tsp paprika
- 1 tsp chili powder
- 1 tsp salt
- 1 egg
- 400 g / 14 oz chicken thighs

Method

1. Preheat your air fryer to 180 °C / 350 °F and line the bottom of the basket with parchment paper.
2. Place the cracks into a mixing bowl and crush them until they resemble breadcrumbs.
3. Add the fresh parsley, paprika, chili powder, and salt. Mix well to fully combine the ingredients.
4. In a separate bowl, crack the egg and whisk well.
5. Dip the chicken thighs into the egg, followed by the crackers and spice mixture. Make sure the thighs are fully covered in breadcrumbs on all sides.
6. Place the chicken thighs into the prepared air fryer basket and cook for 12-15 minutes until golden and crispy.

Sweet and Sticky Air Fryer Meatballs

Makes 4 servings
Preparation time – 30 minutes
Cooking time – 15 minutes
Nutritional values per serving – 257 kcals, 16 g carbs, 19 g protein, 11 g fat

Ingredients

For the meatballs:
- 200 g / 7 oz rolled oats
- 100 g / 3.5 oz crackers
- 2 eggs, beaten
- 1 x 400 ml evaporated milk
- 1 tbsp onion powder
- 1 tbsp garlic powder
- 1 tsp salt
- 1 tbsp ground cumin
- 800 g / 28 oz ground minced beef

For the sauce:
- 4 tbsp brown sugar
- 3 tbsp honey
- 2 tbsp corn starch
- 3 tbsp soy sauce
- 2 tbsp Worcestershire sauce

Simon Brookfield

Method

1. Preheat your air fryer to 180 °C / 350 °F and line the bottom of the basket with parchment paper.
2. To make the meatballs, rolled oats, crackers, eggs, evaporated milk, onion powder, garlic powder, salt, ground cumin. Stir until fully combined.
3. Fold in the beef and mix well.
4. Roll the mixture into small even meatballs. Transfer into the prepared air fryer basket. Close the lid and cook the meatballs for 12-15 until golden and browned.
5. While the meatballs are cooking, make the sauce by combining all of the ingredients well in a saucepan. Heat the mixture until the sauce begins the thicken and is hot all the way through.
6. Serve the meatballs hot with the sweet and sticky sauce over the top. Add some rice and vegetables to turn it into a hearty lunchtime dish.

SIDES
||||||||||||||||||||

Simon Brookfield

Air Fryer Garlic Bread

Makes 8 servings
Preparation time – 5 minutes
Cooking time – 5 minutes
Nutritional values per serving – 137 kcals, 15 g carbs, 4 g protein, 9 g fat

Ingredients

- 4 tbsp butter, softened
- 2 garlic cloves, peeled and minced
- 2 tsp fresh parsley, finely chopped
- 8 slices ciabatta bread
- 3 tbsp Parmesan cheese, grated

Method

1. Preheat your air fryer to 180 °C / 350 °F and line the bottom of the basket with parchment paper.
2. Combine the butter, garlic cloves, and fresh parsley in a bowl.
3. Spread the garlic butter mixture evenly over the 8 ciabatta slices. Top with grated Parmesan cheese.
4. Place the ciabatta slices in the air fryer, close the lid, and cook for 5 minutes until the ciabatta is golden and crispy, and the cheese has melted.

Crispy Air Fryer Chickpeas

Makes 4 servings
Preparation time – 5 minutes
Cooking time – 15 minutes
Nutritional values per serving – 131 kcals, 15 g carbs, 8 g protein, 4 g fat

Ingredients

- 1 x 400 g / 14 oz can chickpeas
- 1 tbsp olive oil
- 1 tsp smoked paprika
- 1 tsp cajun seasoning
- 1 tsp cayenne pepper
- 1 tsp black pepper

Method

1. Preheat your air fryer to 200 °C / 400 °F and line the bottom of the basket with parchment paper.
2. Drain the chickpeas and rinse with cold water. Place them into a large mixing bowl.
3. Stir in the olive oil, smoked paprika, cajun seasoning, cayenne pepper, and black pepper. Toss to fully coat all of the chickpeas in the oil and spices.
4. Transfer the chickpeas to the air fryer and cook for 12-15 minutes until golden and crispy.
5. Serve as part of your favourite vegetables for lunch.

Air Fryer Potatoes

Makes 4 servings
Preparation time – 5 minutes
Cooking time – 15 minutes
Nutritional values per serving – 120 kcals, 19 g carbs, 4 g protein, 5 g fat

Ingredients

- 400 g / 14 oz baby new potatoes, halved
- 1 tbsp olive oil
- 1 tsp garlic powder
- 1 tsp dried mixed herbs
- 1 tsp Cajun powder
- ½ tsp salt
- ½ tsp black pepper

Method

1. Preheat your air fryer to 200 °C / 400 °F and line the bottom of the basket with parchment paper.
2. In a large mixing bowl, mix the potatoes with the olive oil, garlic powder, dried mixed herbs Cajun powder, salt, and pepper.
3. Place potatoes in the prepared basket in your air fryer, close the lid, and cook for 15 minutes.
4. Serve hot as a side to your main meal.

Air Fryer Sweet Potato Fries

Makes 4 servings
Preparation time – 5 minutes
Cooking time – 10 minutes
Nutritional values per serving – 111 kcals, 18 g carbs, 3 g protein, 4 g fat

Ingredients

- 2 sweet potatoes, peeled
- 2 tbsp olive oil
- 1 tsp salt
- 1 tsp black pepper
- 1 tsp paprika
- 1 tsp garlic powder

Method

1. Preheat your air fryer to 200 °C / 400 °F and line the bottom of the basket with parchment paper.
2. Slice the sweet potatoes into wedges and place in a large mixing bowl.
3. Add the olive oil, salt, black pepper, paprika, and garlic powder in the bowl. Toss to coat the potato wedges in the oil and seasoning.
4. Transfer the sweet potato wedges to the air fryer and cook for 10 minutes, turning halfway through, until crispy.

Air Fryer Mixed Vegetables

Makes 4 servings
Preparation time – 10 minutes
Cooking time – 20 minutes
Nutritional values per serving – 99 kcals, 15 g carbs, 3 g protein, 5 g fat

Ingredients

- 100 g / 3.5 oz Brussels sprouts, halved
- 1 aubergine, sliced
- 1 red pepper, sliced
- 2 large carrots, peeled and sliced
- 2 tbsp olive oil
- 1 tbsp balsamic vinegar
- 2 tbsp dried mixed herbs
- ½ tsp salt
- ½ tsp black pepper

Method

1. Preheat your air fryer to 200 °C / 400 °F and line the bottom of the basket with parchment paper.
2. Place the chopped vegetables in a large mixing bowl and toss in the olive oil, balsamic vinegar, dried mixed herbs, salt, and black pepper.
3. Place the vegetables in the air fryer for 15-20 minutes until soft and tender.
4. Serve alongside your main meal.

Air Fryer Broccoli

Makes 2 servings
Preparation time – 10 minutes
Cooking time – 10 minutes
Nutritional values per serving – 65 kcals, 5 g carbs, 2 g protein, 4 g fat

Ingredients

- 1 broccoli, broken into florets
- 1 tbsp olive oil
- 1 clove garlic, peeled and minced
- 1 tsp salt
- 1 tsp black pepper

Method

1. Preheat your air fryer to 180 °C / 350 °F and line the bottom of the basket with parchment paper.
2. Place the broccoli florets in a bowl and add the olive oil, garlic, salt, and black pepper. Toss to fully coat the broccoli.
3. Add the broccoli to the air fryer and cook for 10 minutes until tender.

Air Fryer Buffalo Cauliflower with Blue Cheese Sauce

Makes 2 servings
Preparation time – 10 minutes
Cooking time – 15 minutes
Nutritional values per serving – 167 kcals, 10 g carbs, 4 g protein, 9 g fat

Ingredients

For the cauliflower:

- 1 cauliflower, broken into florets
- 3 tbsp hot sauce
- 3 tbsp butter, melted
- ½ tsp garlic powder
- ½ tsp salt
- ½ tsp black pepper
- 1 tbsp corn starch

For the blue cheese sauce:

- 50 g / 1.8 oz blue cheese, crumbled
- 2 tbsp sour cream
- 3 tbsp mayonnaise
- ½ tsp salt
- ½ tsp black pepper

Method

1. Preheat your air fryer to 180 °C / 350 °F and line the bottom of the basket with parchment paper.
2. In a large mixing bowl, mix the hot sauce, melted butter, garlic powder, salt, and black pepper. Add the cauliflower to the bowl and toss to coat.
3. Sprinkle the corn starch over the cauliflower and mix well.
4. Place the cauliflower into the prepared basket in the air fryer machine, close the lid, and cook for 15 minutes until golden and crispy.
5. While the cauliflower is cooking, make the blue cheese sauce. Mix all of the ingredients together in a small bowl.
6. When the cauliflower is cooked, remove from the air fryer, and serve with the blue cheese sauce on the side.

Air Fryer Honey Carrots

Makes 4 servings
Preparation time – 10 minutes
Cooking time – 15 minutes
Nutritional values per serving – 120 kcals, 13 g carbs, 4 g protein, 5 g fat

Ingredients

- 4 large carrots, peeled and chopped
- 1 tbsp olive oil
- 2 tbsp honey
- 1 tsp black pepper

Method

1. Preheat your air fryer to 150 °C / 300 °F and line the bottom of the basket with parchment paper.
2. Place the chopped carrots in a bowl and top with the olive oil, honey, and black pepper. Toss to fully coat the carrots.
3. Transfer the carrots to the lined air fryer basket, shut the lid, and cook for 20 minutes until the carrots are soft in the centre but crispy on the edges.

Air Fryer Fried Rice

Makes 4 servings
Preparation time – 5 minutes
Cooking time – 15 minutes
Nutritional values per serving – 201 kcals, 15 g carbs, 10 g protein, 6 g fat

Ingredients

- 400 g / 14 oz cooked brown rice
- 100 g / 3.5 oz frozen mixed vegetables
- 1 tbsp olive oil
- 2 eggs, scrambled

Method

1. Preheat your air fryer to 150 °C / 300 °F and line the bottom of the basket with parchment paper.
2. Place the cooked rice in a bowl and mix in the frozen vegetables.
3. Drizzle the olive oil over the rice and toss to coat. Add the scrambled eggs.
4. Transfer the rice mixture into the prepared air fryer and cook for 15 minutes.

Simon Brookfield

Crispy Cinnamon French Toast

Makes 2 servings
Preparation time – 10 minutes
Cooking time – 5 minutes
Nutritional values per serving – 231 kcals, 18 g carbs, 7 g protein, 10 g fat

Ingredients

- 4 slices white bread
- 4 eggs
- 200 ml milk (cow's milk, cashew milk, soy milk, or oat milk)
- 2 tbsp granulated sugar
- 1 tsp brown sugar
- 1 tsp vanilla extract
- ½ tsp ground cinnamon

Method

1. Preheat your air fryer to 150 °C / 300 °F and line the bottom of the basket with parchment paper.
2. Cut each of the bread slices into 2 even rectangles and set them aside.
3. In a mixing bowl, whisk together the 4 eggs, milk, granulated sugar, brown sugar, vanilla extract, and ground cinnamon.
4. Soak the bread pieces in the egg mixture until they are fully covered and soaked in the mixture.
5. Place the coated bread slices in the lined air fryer, close the lid, and cook for 4-5 minutes until the bread is crispy and golden.
6. Serve the French toast slices with whatever toppings you desire.

Air Fryer Eggy Bread

Makes 2 servings
Preparation time – 5 minutes
Cooking time – 5-7 minutes
Nutritional values per serving – 267 kcals, 24 g carbs, 15 g protein, 18 g fat

Ingredients

- 4 slices white bread
- 4 eggs, beaten
- 1 tsp black pepper
- 1 tsp dried chives

Method

1. Preheat your air fryer to 150 °C / 300 °F and line the bottom of the basket with parchment paper.
2. Whisk the eggs in a large mixing bowl and soak each slice of bread until fully coated.
3. Transfer the eggy bread to the preheated air fryer and cook for 5-7 minutes until the eggs are set and the bread is crispy.
4. Serve hot with a sprinkle of black pepper and chives on top.

Egg Fried Rice

Makes 2 servings
Preparation time – 5 minutes
Cooking time – 15 minutes
Nutritional values per serving – 198 kcals, 21 g carbs, 11 g protein, 7 g fat

Ingredients

- 400 g / 14 oz cooked white or brown rice
- 100 g / 3.5 oz fresh peas and sweetcorn
- 2 tbsp olive oil
- 2 eggs, scrambled

Method

1. Preheat the air fryer to 150 °C / 300 °F and line the bottom of the basket with parchment paper.
2. In a bowl, mix the cooked white or brown rice and the fresh peas and sweetcorn.
3. Pour in 2 tbsp olive oil and toss to coat evenly. Stir in the scrambled eggs.
4. Transfer the egg rice into the lined air fryer basket, close the lid, and cook for 15 minutes until the eggs are cooked and the rice is soft.
5. Serve as a side dish with some cooked meat or tofu.

Cauliflower with Hot Sauce and Blue Cheese Sauce

Makes 2 servings
Preparation time – 10 minutes
Cooking time – 15 minutes
Nutritional values per serving – 143 kcals, 9 g carbs, 2 g protein, 5 g fat

Ingredients

For the cauliflower:
- 1 cauliflower, broken into florets
- 4 tbsp hot sauce
- 2 tbsp olive oil
- 1 tsp garlic powder
- ½ tsp salt
- ½ tsp black pepper
- 1 tbsp plain flour
- 1 tbsp corn starch

For the blue cheese sauce:
- 50 g / 1.8 oz blue cheese, crumbled
- 2 tbsp sour cream
- 2 tbsp mayonnaise
- ½ tsp salt
- ½ tsp black pepper

Simon Brookfield

Method

1. Preheat the air fryer to 180 °C / 350 °F and line the bottom of the basket with parchment paper.
2. In a bowl, combine the hot sauce, olive oil, garlic powder, salt, and black pepper until it forms a consistent mixture. Add the cauliflower to the bowl and coat in the sauce.
3. Stir in the plain flour and corn starch until well combined.
4. Transfer the cauliflower to the lined basket in the air fryer, close the lid, and cook for 12-15 minutes until the cauliflower has softened and is golden in colour.
5. Meanwhile, make the blue cheese sauce by combining all of the ingredients. When the cauliflower is ready, remove it from the air fryer and serve with the blue cheese sauce on the side.

Sweet Potato Wedges

Makes 4 servings
Preparation time – 10 minutes
Cooking time – 20 minutes
Nutritional values per serving – 112 kcals, 14 g carbs, 9 g protein, 5 g fat

Ingredients

- ½ tsp garlic powder
- ½ tsp cumin
- ½ tsp smoked paprika
- ½ tsp cayenne pepper
- ½ tsp salt
- ½ tsp black pepper
- 1 tsp dried chives
- 4 tbsp olive oil
- 3 large sweet potatoes, cut into wedges

Method

1. Preheat the air fryer to 180 °C / 350 °F and line the bottom of the basket with parchment paper.
2. In a bowl, mix the garlic powder, cumin, smoked paprika, cayenne pepper, salt, black pepper, and dried chives until combined.
3. Whisk in the olive oil and coat the sweet potato wedges in the spicy oil mixture.
4. Transfer the coated sweet potatoes to the air fryer and close the lid. Cook for 20 minutes until cooked and crispy. Serve hot as a side with your main meal.

Homemade Croquettes

Makes 4 servings
Preparation time – 15 minutes
Cooking time – 15 minutes
Nutritional values per serving – 306 kcals, 20 g carbs, 5 g protein, 7 g fat

Ingredients

- 400 g / 14 oz white rice, uncooked
- 1 onion, sliced
- 2 cloves garlic, finely sliced
- 2 eggs, beaten
- 50 g / 3.5 oz parmesan cheese, grated
- 1 tsp salt
- 1 tsp black pepper
- 50 g / 3.5 oz breadcrumbs
- 1 tsp dried oregano

Method

1. In a large mixing bowl, combine the white rice, onion slices, garlic cloves slices, one beaten egg, parmesan cheese, and a sprinkle of salt and pepper.
2. Whisk the second egg in a separate bowl and place the breadcrumbs into another bowl.
3. Shape the mixture into 12 even croquettes and roll evenly in the egg, followed by the breadcrumbs.
4. Preheat the air fryer to 190 °C / 375 °F and line the bottom of the basket with parchment paper.
5. Place the croquettes in the lined air fryer basket and cook for 15 minutes, turning halfway through, until crispy and golden. Enjoy while hot as a side to your main dish.

Sweet and Sticky Parsnips and Carrots

Makes 2 servings
Preparation time – 10 minutes
Cooking time – 15 minutes
Nutritional values per serving – 99 kcals, 9 g carbs, 3 g protein, 2 g fat

Ingredients

- 4 large carrots, peeled and chopped into long chunks
- 4 large parsnips, peeled and chopped into long chunks
- 1 tbsp olive oil
- 2 tbsp honey
- 1 tsp dried mixed herbs

Method

1. Preheat the air fryer to 150 °C / 300 °F and line the bottom of the basket with parchment paper.
2. Place the chopped carrots and parsnips in a large bowl and drizzle over the olive oil and honey. Sprinkle in some black pepper to taste and toss well to fully coat the vegetables.
3. Transfer the coated vegetables into the air fryer basket and shut the lid. Cook for 20 minutes until the carrots and parsnips and cooked and crispy.
4. Serve as a side with your dinner.

BBQ Beetroot Crisps

Makes 4 servings
Preparation time – 5 minutes
Cooking time – 5 minutes
Nutritional values per serving – 78 kcals, 11 g carbs, 5 g protein, 9 g fat

Ingredients

- 400 g / 14 oz beetroot, sliced
- 2 tbsp olive oil
- 1 tbsp BBQ seasoning
- ½ tsp black pepper

Method

1. Preheat the air fryer to 180 °C / 350 °F and line the bottom of the basket with parchment paper.
2. Place the beetroot slices in a large bowl. Add the olive oil, BBQ seasoning, and black pepper, and toss to coat the beetroot slices on both sides.
3. Place the beetroot slices in the air fryer and cook for 5 minutes until hot and crispy.

Cheesy Broccoli

Makes 4 servings
Preparation time – 10 minutes
Cooking time – 5 minutes
Nutritional values per serving – 99 kcals, 4 g carbs, 2 g protein, 4 g fat

Ingredients

- 1 large broccoli head, broken into florets
- 4 tbsp soft cheese
- 1 tsp black pepper
- 50 g / 3.5 oz cheddar cheese, grated

Method

1. Preheat the air fryer to 150 °C / 300 °F and line the mesh basket with parchment paper or grease it with olive oil.
2. Wash and drain the broccoli florets and place in a bowl and stir in the soft cheese and black pepper to fully coat all of the florets.
3. Transfer the broccoli to the air fryer basket and sprinkle the cheddar cheese on top. Close the lid and cook for 5-7 minutes until the broccoli has softened and the cheese has melted.
4. Serve as a side dish to your favourite meal.

Simon Brookfield

BEEF AND PORK

Sausage Burritos

Makes 4 servings
Preparation time – 20 minutes
Cooking time – 20 minutes
Nutritional values per serving – 450 kcals, 31 g carbs, 10 g protein, 12 g fat

Ingredients

- 1 medium sweet potato
- 2 tbsp olive oil
- 1 tsp salt
- 1 tsp black pepper
- 8 sausages, uncooked
- 4 white flour tortillas
- 4 eggs, beaten
- 200 ml milk (any kind)
- 100 g / 3.5 oz cheddar cheese, grated

Method

1. Preheat the air fryer to 200 °C / 400 °F and line the air fryer mesh basket with parchment paper.
2. Peel the sweet potato and cut it into small chunks.
3. Place the sweet potato chunks in a bowl and toss in 1 tbsp olive oil. Sprinkle salt and pepper over the top.
4. Transfer the sweet potato chunks into the air fryer and cook for 8-10 minutes until hot. Remove from the air fryer and set aside to drain on paper towels.
5. Heat 1 tbsp olive oil in a medium frying pan and cook the sausages for 5-7 minutes until slightly browned. Remove the sausages and set them aside on paper towels to drain.
6. In a bowl, whisk together the beaten eggs and milk, and pour into the hot frying pan. Cook the eggs and use a fork to scramble them as they cook in the pan.
7. Once the eggs are cooked, mix them with the potatoes, sausages, and cheddar cheese in a bowl.
8. Spread the mixture evenly across the 4 white flour tortillas and roll them each up into tight burritos. Use a toothpick to keep them together if necessary.
9. Place the burritos into the hot air fryer and cook for 6-8 minutes, turning them over halfway through.
10. Enjoy the burritos for breakfast or lunch.

Crispy Chili Sausages

Makes 4 servings
Preparation time – 10 minutes
Cooking time – 20 minutes
Nutritional values per serving – 245 kcals, 5 g carbs, 10 g protein, 13 g fat

Ingredients

- 8 sausages, uncooked
- 2 eggs
- ½ tsp salt
- ½ black pepper
- ½ tsp chili flakes
- ½ tsp paprika

Method

1. Preheat the air fryer to 180 °C / 350 °F and line the bottom of the basket with parchment paper.
2. Place the sausages in the air fryer and cook for 5 minutes until slightly browned, but not fully cooked. Remove from the air fryer and set aside.
3. While the sausages are cooking, whisk together the eggs, salt, black pepper, chili flakes, and paprika. Coat the sausages evenly in the egg and spice mixture.
4. Return the sausages to the air fryer and cook for a further 5 minutes until brown and crispy.
5. Eat the sausages while hot with a side of steamed vegetables or place them in a sandwich for lunch.

Beef Stroganoff

Makes 4 servings
Preparation time – 20 minutes
Cooking time – 20 minutes
Nutritional values per serving – 398 kcals, 17 g carbs, 31 g protein, 17 g fat

Ingredients

- 4 cubes / 800 ml beef stock cubes
- 4 tbsp olive oil
- 1 onion, chopped
- 200 g / 7 oz sour cream
- 200 g / 7 oz mushroom, finely sliced
- 500 g / 17.6 oz steak, chopped
- 4 x 100 g / 3.5 oz egg noodles, cooked

Method

1. Preheat the air fryer to 200 °C / 400 °F and line the bottom of the basket with parchment paper.
2. Boil 800 ml of water and use it to dissolve the 4 beef stock cubes.
3. In a heat-proof bowl, mix the olive oil, onion, sour cream, mushrooms, and beef stock until fully combined.
4. Coat all sides of the steak chunks in the mixture and set aside to marinate for 10 minutes.
5. Transfer the steak to the air fryer, close the lid, and cook for 10 minutes. Serve the steak hot with a serving of egg noodles.

Beef Satay

Makes 4 servings
Preparation time – 20 minutes
Cooking time – 10 minutes
Nutritional values per serving – 184 kcals, 5 g carbs, 17 g protein, 12 g fat

Ingredients

- 500 g / 17.6 oz beef, cubed
- 2 tbsp soy sauce
- 2 tbsp fish sauce
- 2 tbsp hot sauce
- 2 tbsp brown sugar
- 2 tsp garlic powder
- 2 tsp ground ginger
- 2 tsp ground cumin
- 50 g / 1.8 oz roasted peanuts, chopped

Method

1. Preheat the air fryer to 200 °C / 400 °F and line the bottom of the basket with parchment paper.
2. Place the beef cubes in a large bowl. In a separate bowl, mix the soy sauce, fish sauce, hot sauce, brown sugar, garlic powder, ground ginger, and ground cumin in a bowl until fully combined.
3. Coat the beef cubes in the sauce and spice mixture until all sides are covered. Cover the bowl with a clean tea towel or tin foil and allow to marinate for 10 minutes.
4. Transfer the beef chunks to the air fryer and cook for 10 minutes until browned and crispy.
5. Serve the beef satay topped with roasted peanuts and enjoy!

Homemade Crispy Pepperoni Pizza

Makes 4 servings
Preparation time – 15 minutes
Cooking time – 10 minutes
Nutritional values per serving – 213 kcals, 15 g carbs, 9 g protein, 8 g fat

Ingredients

For the pizza dough:

- 500 g / 17.6 oz plain flour
- 1 tsp salt
- 1 tsp dry non-fast-acting yeast
- 400 ml warm water

For the toppings:

- 100 g / 3.5 oz tomato sauce
- 100 g / 3.5 oz mozzarella cheese, grated
- 8 slices pepperoni

Method

1. To make the pizza dough, place the plain flour, salt, and dry yeast in a large mixing bowl. Pour in the warm water bit by bit until it forms a tacky dough.
2. Lightly dust a clean kitchen top surface with plain flour and roll the dough out until it is around ½ an inch thick.
3. Preheat your air fryer to 150 °C / 300 °F and line the bottom of the basket with parchment paper.
4. Spread the tomato sauce evenly across the dough and top with grated mozzarella cheese. Top with the pepperoni slices and carefully transfer the pizza into the lined air fryer basket.
5. Cook the pizza until the crust is golden and crispy, and the mozzarella cheese has melted.
6. Enjoy the pizza while still hot with a side salad and some potato wedges.

Pulled Pork, Bacon, and Cheese Sliders

Makes 2 servings
Preparation time – 20 minutes
Cooking time – 30 minutes
Nutritional values per serving – 245 kcals, 6 g carbs, 15 g protein, 9 g fat

Ingredients

- 2 x 50 g / 3.5 oz pork steaks
- 1 tsp salt
- 1 tsp black pepper
- 4 slices bacon strips, chopped into small pieces
- 1 tbsp soy sauce
- 1 tbsp BBQ sauce
- 100 g / 7 oz cheddar cheese, grated
- 2 bread buns

Method

1. Preheat the air fryer to 200 °C / 400 °F and line the bottom of the basket with parchment paper.
2. Place the pork steaks on a clean surface and season with salt and black pepper. Move the pork steak in the prepared air fryer basket and cook for 15 minutes.
3. Remove the steak from the air fryer and shred using two forks. Mix with the chopped bacon in a heatproof bowl and place the bowl in the air fryer. Cook for 10 minutes.
4. Remove the bowl from the air fryer and stir in the soy sauce and BBQ sauce. Return the bowl to the air fryer basket and continue cooking for a further 5 minutes.
5. Meanwhile, spread the cheese across one half of the bread buns. Top with the cooked pulled pork and an extra squirt of BBQ sauce.

The Complete XXL Air Fryer Cookbook UK

Sweet and Sticky Ribs

Makes 2 servings
Preparation time – 10 minutes
Cooking time – 1 hour 15 minutes
Nutritional values per serving – 298 kcals, 5 g carbs, 23 g protein, 21 g fat

Ingredients

- 500 g / 17.6 oz pork ribs
- 2 cloves garlic, minced
- 2 tbsp soy sauce
- 2 tsp honey
- 1 tbsp cayenne pepper
- 1 tsp olive oil
- 2 tbsp BBQ sauce
- 1 tsp salt
- 1 tsp black pepper

Method

1. Place the pork ribs on a clean surface and cut them into smaller chunks if necessary.
2. In a small mixing bowl, combine the minced garlic, soy sauce, 1 tsp honey, cayenne pepper, olive oil, BBQ sauce, salt, and pepper. Rub the pork ribs into the sauce and spice the mixture until fully coated.
3. Place the coated ribs in the fridge for 1 hour. Meanwhile, preheat the air fryer to 180 °C / 350 °F and line the bottom of the basket with parchment paper.
4. After one hour, transfer the pork ribs into the prepared air fryer basket. Close the lid and cook for 15 minutes, using tongs to turn them halfway through.
5. Once cooked, remove the ribs from the air fryer and use a brush to top each rib with the remaining 1 tsp honey.
6. Return the ribs to the air fryer for a further 2-3 minutes to heat the honey glaze before serving.

POULTRY AND FISH

Air Fryer BBQ and Cheddar Chicken

Makes 4 servings
Preparation time – 15 minutes
Cooking time – 10 minutes
Nutritional values per serving – 314 kcals, 17 g carbs, 21 g protein, 13 g fat

Ingredients

- 4 slices white bread
- 4 x 100 g / 3.5 oz skinless, boneless chicken breast fillets
- 1 tsp salt
- 1 tsp black pepper
- 50 g / 1.8 oz cheddar cheese, grated
- 1 tsp garlic powder
- 1 tsp dried mixed herbs
- 100 g / 3.5 oz plain flour
- 2 eggs, beaten
- 4 tbsp smoky BBQ sauce

The Complete XXL Air Fryer Cookbook UK

Method

1. Preheat your air fryer to 200 °C / 400 °F and line the bottom of the basket with parchment paper.
2. Cut the crusts off each slice of bread and place the bread into a food processor. Blend for 20 seconds or until the bread is fully broken up into crumbs. Transfer the breadcrumbs into a bowl and set aside.
3. Cut the chicken breast fillets in half and season with salt and pepper.
4. In a mixing bowl, mix the cheddar cheese, garlic powder, and mixed herbs until fully combined.
5. Spoon the cheese evenly onto the chicken breasts and fold the fillets over. Press the edges of the fillets down to seal in the cheese mixture.
6. In separate bowls, place the flour and beaten eggs.
7. Coat the chicken breasts first in the flour, then in the egg mixture, and finally, cover them in the homemade breadcrumbs. By the end, the chicken breasts should be fully coated in the breadcrumbs.
8. Transfer the coated chicken breasts into the prepared air fryer basket, close the lid, and cook the fillets for 10 minutes until crispy and golden.
9. Serve the chicken hot with a squirt of BBQ sauce on top.

Simon Brookfield

Air Fryer Chicken Wings

Makes 4 servings
Preparation time – 10 minutes
Cooking time – 20 minutes
Nutritional values per serving – 213 kcals, 12 g carbs, 11 g protein, 10 g fat

Ingredients

- 400 g / 14 oz chicken wings
- 1 tsp black pepper
- 1 tsp garlic powder
- 4 tbsp hot sauce
- 2 tbsp soy sauce
- 4 tbsp olive oil

Method

1. Preheat the air fryer to 200 °C / 400 °F and line the bottom of the basket with parchment paper.
2. Season the wings with black pepper and garlic powder. Cook in the air fryer for 10-12 minutes until they turn slightly brown.
3. While the chicken wings are in the air fryer, whisk together the hot sauce, soy sauce, and olive oil in a bowl until fully combined into a smooth sauce.
4. Remove the chicken wings from the air fryer and coat them in the sauce.
5. Return the wings to the hot air fryer and cook for 5-7 minutes until hot and crispy.
6. Serve the wings hot with a side of salad or cooked veggies.

Southern Fried Crispy Air Fryer Chicken

Makes 4 servings
Preparation time – 15 minutes
Cooking time – 15 minutes
Nutritional values per serving – 344 kcals, 15 g carbs, 25 g protein, 15 g fat

Ingredients

- 200 g / 7 oz plain crackers
- 1 tsp fresh basil, finely chopped
- 1 tsp smoked paprika
- 1 tsp BBQ seasoning
- 1 tsp chili flakes
- 1 tsp black pepper
- 1 tsp salt
- 1 egg
- 400 g / 14 oz chicken thighs

Method

1. Preheat the air fryer to 180 °C / 350 °F and line the bottom of the basket with parchment paper.
2. Crush the crackers up in a mixing bowl until they resemble breadcrumbs.
3. Stir in the fresh basil, smoked paprika, BBQ seasoning, chili flakes, black pepper, and salt. Mix the ingredients until fully combined.
4. In a new bowl, whisk the egg well. Dip each of the chicken thighs into the egg to fully coat. Roll the coated chicken thighs around in the spicy cracker mixture until fully coated on all sides.
5. Place the chicken thighs into the lined air fryer basket and cook for 12-15 minutes until golden and crispy.

Air Fryer BBQ Chicken

Makes 4 servings
Preparation time – 10 minutes
Cooking time – 25 minutes
Nutritional values per serving – 334 kcals, 15 g carbs, 9 g protein, 20 g fat

Ingredients

- 1 tsp cumin
- 1 tsp smoked paprika
- 1 tsp BBQ seasoning
- 1 tsp garlic powder
- 1 tsp salt
- 1 tsp black pepper
- 4 x 100 g / 3.5 oz chicken breast fillets
- 8 tbsp BBQ sauce

Method

1. Preheat the air fryer to 200 °C / 400 °F and line the bottom of the basket with parchment paper.
2. Place the cumin, smoked paprika, BBQ seasoning, garlic powder, salt, and black pepper in a bowl until fully combined.
3. Coat the chicken in the spice mixture and place into the air fryer with the plain side down. Close the lid of the machine and cook for 20 minutes.
4. Remove the chicken breasts from the air fryer and brush the top of each fillet with BBQ sauce. Return to the air fryer basket and cook for a further 5 minutes until the sauce is hot.
5. Enjoy with a side of cooked vegetables.

Turkey Meatballs

Makes 4 servings
Preparation time – 10 minutes
Cooking time – 10 minutes
Nutritional values per serving – 299 kcals, 15 g carbs, 22 g protein, 11 g fat

Ingredients

- 400 g / 14 oz ground turkey
- 1 tsp cajun seasoning
- 1 tsp onion powder
- 1 tsp garlic powder
- 2 tbsp dried oregano
- ½ tsp salt
- ½ tsp black pepper
- 1 egg, beaten
- 1 tbsp soy sauce

Method

1. Preheat the air fryer to 200 °C / 400 °F and line the bottom of the basket with parchment paper.
2. In a large bowl, mix the ground turkey, cajun seasoning, onion powder, garlic powder, dried oregano, salt, and black pepper in a bowl until well combined.
3. Whisk in the beaten egg and soy sauce. Fold the mixture together until well combined.
4. Use a spoon to scoop the mixture into small meatballs and place them into the lined air fryer basket. Cook for 12-15 minutes until browned and crispy.
5. Serve while the meatballs are still hot with some spaghetti or in a large bread roll with some sauce.

Air Fryer Tuna and Sweetcorn Sandwiches

Makes 2 servings
Preparation time – 10 minutes
Cooking time – 5 minutes
Nutritional values per serving – 300 kcals, 23 g carbs, 10 g protein, 15 g fat

Ingredients

- 4 slices white or wholemeal bread
- 2 x 200 g / 7 oz canned tuna, drained
- 4 tbsp mayonnaise
- 200 g / 7 oz mozzarella cheese, grated
- 50 g / 1.8 oz sweetcorn

Method

1. Preheat the air fryer to 180 °C / 350 °F and line the air fryer mesh basket with parchment paper.
2. Lay the sandwich slices out on a clean surface.
3. In a mixing bowl, combine the tuna, mayonnaise, mozzarella cheese, and sweetcorn until a smooth mixture is formed.
4. Spread the tuna mayo mixture evenly across two slices of bread and top each one with a remaining slice of bread to form two sandwiches.
5. Place the sandwiches in the preheated air fryer and cook for 5 minutes, turning halfway through, until the bread is crispy, and the cheese has melted.

Crispy Salmon

Makes 2 servings
Preparation time – 10 minutes
Cooking time – 10 minutes
Nutritional values per serving – 112 kcals, 5 g carbs, 18 g protein, 17 g fat

Ingredients

- 2 x 100 g / 3.5 oz fillets salmon
- 1 tsp olive oil
- ½ tsp salt
- ½ tsp black pepper
- Juice 1 lemon

Method

1. Preheat the air fryer to 180 °C / 350 °F and line the air fryer mesh basket with parchment paper.
2. Rinse the salmon fillets and pat dry with paper towels.
3. Lightly coat the fillets on both sides with olive oil and top one side with salt, black pepper, and the juice of 1 lemon.
4. Place the salmon fillets in the air fryer with the seasoned side up. Close the lid and cook the salmon fillets for 10 minutes, turning halfway through.

Tuna Patties

Makes 2 servings
Preparation time – 40 minutes
Cooking time – 10 minutes
Nutritional values per serving – 247 kcals, 11 g carbs, 21 g protein, 8 g fat

Ingredients

- 200 g / 7 oz canned tuna
- 2 tbsp plain flour
- 2 eggs, beaten
- 100 ml milk (any kind)
- 1 onion, sliced
- 1 tsp chili powder
- 1 tsp black pepper

Method

1. In a large mixing bowl, mix all of the ingredients together until fully combined. Shape the mixture into circular patties.
2. Place the patties on a lined baking tray and leave in the fridge for 30 minutes.
3. Preheat the air fryer to 180 °C / 350 °F and line the air fryer mesh basket with parchment paper.
4. Transfer the patties into the air fryer and close the lid. Cook for 8-10 minutes until hot.

Sticky Soy Sauce and Ginger Glazed Cod

Makes 2 servings
Preparation time – 10 minutes
Cooking time – 5 minutes
Nutritional values per serving – 169 kcals, 4 g carbs, 20 g protein, 6 g fat

Ingredients

- 2 x 100 g / 3.5 oz cod fillets
- 1 tbsp olive oil
- 1 tbsp soy sauce
- 1 tsp dried ginger
- 1 tsp honey
- 1 tsp salt
- 1 tsp black pepper

Method

1. Preheat the air fryer to 180 °C / 350 °F and line the air fryer mesh basket with parchment paper.
2. Lay the cod fillets out on a clean surface.
3. In a bowl, place the olive oil, soy sauce, dried ginger, honey, salt, and black pepper in a bowl.
4. Coat the cod fillets in the spicy sauce and transfer to the lined air fryer basket. Cook for 8-10 minutes, turning halfway through.
5. Serve while the cod is still hot with a side salad.

Simon Brookfield

VEGETARIAN AND VEGAN

Roasted Vegetable Pasta

Makes 4 servings
Preparation time – 10 minutes
Cooking time – 15 minutes
Nutritional values per serving – 387 kcals, 60 g carbs, 10 g protein, 15 g fat

Ingredients

- 400 g / 14 oz penne pasta
- 1 courgette, sliced
- 1 red pepper, deseeded and sliced
- 100 g / 3.5 oz mushroom, sliced
- 2 tbsp olive oil
- 1 tsp Italian seasoning
- 200 g cherry tomatoes, halved
- 2 tbsp fresh basil, chopped
- ½ tsp black pepper

Method

1. Cook the pasta according to the packet instructions.
2. Preheat the air fryer to 190 °C / 370 °F and line the air fryer with parchment paper or grease it with olive oil.
3. In a bowl, place the courgette, pepper, and mushroom, and toss in 2 tbsp olive oil
4. Place the vegetables in the air fryer and cook for 15 minutes.
5. Once the vegetables have softened, mix with the penne pasta, chopped cherry tomatoes, and fresh basil.
6. Serve while hot with a sprinkle of black pepper in each dish.

Spinach and Egg Air Fryer Breakfast Muffins

Makes 4 servings
Preparation time – 10 minutes
Cooking time – 10 minutes
Nutritional values per serving – 181 kcals, 12 g carbs, 9 g protein, 9 g fat

Ingredients

- 8 eggs
- 100 g / 3.5 oz fresh spinach
- 50 g / 1.8 oz cheddar cheese, grated
- ½ onion, finely sliced
- 1 tsp black pepper

Method

1. Preheat your air fryer to 200 °C / 400 °F and line an 8-pan muffin tray with parchment paper or grease with olive oil.
2. Gently press the spinach leaves into the bottom of each prepared muffin cup.
3. Sprinkle the finely sliced onion on top of the spinach.
4. Crack 2 eggs into each cup on top of the spinach and add some of the grated cheddar cheese on top of the eggs. Top with a light sprinkle of black pepper.
5. Carefully place the muffins into the air fryer basket and shut the lid. Bake for 10 minutes until the eggs are set and the muffins are hot throughout.
6. Serve the muffins while still hot for breakfast.

Vegan Meatballs

Makes 4 servings
Preparation time – 15 minutes
Cooking time – 15 minutes
Nutritional values per serving – 312 kcals, 30 g carbs, 17 g protein, 18 g fat

Ingredients

- 2 tbsp olive oil
- 2 tbsp soy sauce
- 1 onion, finely sliced
- 1 large carrot, peeled and grated
- 1 x 400 g / 14 oz can chickpeas, drained and rinsed
- 50 g / 1.8 oz plain flour
- 50 g / 1.8 oz rolled oats
- 2 tbsp roasted cashews, chopped
- 1 tsp garlic powder
- ½ tsp cumin

Method

1. Preheat the air fryer to 175 °C / 350 °F and line the air fryer with parchment paper or grease it with olive oil.
2. In a large mixing bowl, combine the olive oil and soy sauce. Add the onion slices and grated carrot and toss to coat in the sauce.
3. Place the vegetables in the air fryer and cook for 5 minutes until slightly soft.
4. Meanwhile, place the chickpeas, plain flour, rolled oats, and roasted cashews in a blender, and mix until well combined.
5. Remove the mixture from the blender and stir in the garlic powder and cumin. Add the onions and carrots to the bowl and mix well.
6. Scoop the mixture into small meatballs and place them into the air fryer. Increase the temperature on the machine up to 190 °C / 370 °F and cook the meatballs for 10-12 minutes until golden and crispy.

Spring Ratatouille

Makes 2 servings
Preparation time – 15 minutes
Cooking time – 15 minutes
Nutritional values per serving – 161 kcals, 20 g carbs, 5 g protein, 8 g fat

Ingredients

- 1 tbsp olive oil
- 4 Roma tomatoes, sliced
- 2 cloves garlic, minced
- 1 courgette, cut into chunks
- 1 red pepper and 1 yellow pepper, cut into chunks
- 2 tbsp mixed herbs
- 1 tbsp vinegar

Method

1. Preheat the air fryer to 190 °C / 370 °F and line the air fryer with parchment paper or grease it with olive oil.
2. Place all of the ingredients into a large mixing bowl and mix until fully combined.
3. Transfer the vegetables into the lined air fryer basket, close the lid, and cook for 15 minutes until the vegetables have softened.

Sticky Tofu With Cauliflower Rice

Makes 4 servings
Preparation time – 15 minutes
Cooking time – 20 minutes
Nutritional values per serving – 145 kcals, 18 g carbs, 10 g protein, 18 g fat

Ingredients

For the tofu:

- 1 x 180 g / 6 oz block firm tofu
- 2 tbsp soy sauce
- 1 onion, sliced
- 1 large carrot, peeled and thinly sliced

For the cauliflower:

- 200 g / 7 oz cauliflower florets
- 2 tbsp soy sauce
- 1 tbsp sesame oil
- 2 cloves garlic, minced
- 100 g / 3.5 oz broccoli, chopped into small florets

Method

1. Preheat the air fryer to 190 °C / 370 °F and line the air fryer with parchment paper or grease it with olive oil.
2. Crumble the tofu into a bowl and mix in the soy sauce, and the sliced onion and carrot.
3. Cook the tofu and vegetables in the air fryer for 10 minutes.
4. Meanwhile, place the cauliflower florets into a blender and pulse until it forms a rice-like consistency.
5. Place the cauliflower rice in a bowl and mix in the soy sauce, sesame oil, minced garlic cloves, and broccoli florets until well combined. Transfer to the air fryer and cook for 10 minutes until hot and crispy.

Chickpea and Sweetcorn Falafel

Makes 4 servings
Preparation time – 10 minutes
Cooking time – 15 minutes
Nutritional values per serving – 165 kcals, 10 g carbs, 9 g protein, 9 g fat

Ingredients

- ½ onion, sliced
- 2 cloves garlic, peeled and sliced
- 2 tbsp fresh parsley, chopped
- 2 tbsp fresh coriander, chopped
- 2 x 400 g / 14 oz chickpeas, drained and rinsed
- 1 tsp salt
- 1 tsp black pepper
- 1 tsp baking powder
- 1 tsp dried mixed herbs
- 1 tsp cumin
- 1 tsp chili powder
- 50 g / 1.8 oz sweetcorn, fresh or frozen

The Complete XXL Air Fryer Cookbook UK

Method

1. Preheat the air fryer to 180 °C / 350 °F and line the bottom of the basket with parchment paper.
2. In a food processor, place the onion, garlic cloves, fresh parsley, and fresh coriander. Pulse the ingredients in 30-second intervals until they form a smooth mixture. Scrape the mixture from the sides of the food processor in between each interval if necessary.
3. Mix in the chickpeas, salt, black pepper, baking powder, dried mixed herbs, cumin, and chili powder. Pulse the mixture until fully combined and smooth. Add more water if the mixture is looking a bit dry. The mixture should be dry but not crumbly.
4. Use a spoon to scoop out 2 tbsp of the chickpea mixture at a time and roll into small, even falafels.
5. Transfer the falafels into the prepared air fryer basket and cook for 12-15 minutes.
6. Serve the falafels either hot or cold as a side dish to your main meal or as part of a large salad.

Air Fryer Cheese Sandwich

Makes 2 servings
Preparation time – 10 minutes
Cooking time – 10 minutes
Nutritional values per serving – 234 kcals, 21 g carbs, 7 g protein, 8 g fat

Ingredients

- 4 slices white or wholemeal bread
- 2 tbsp butter
- 50 g / 3.5 oz cheddar cheese, grated

Method

1. Preheat the air fryer to 180 °C / 350 °F and line the bottom of the basket with parchment paper.
2. Lay the slices of bread out on a clean surface and butter one side of each. Evenly sprinkle the cheese on two of the slices and cover with the final two slices.
3. Transfer the sandwiches to the air fryer, close the lid, and cook for 5 minutes until the bread is crispy and golden, and the cheese is melted.

Spinach and Feta Croissants

Makes 4 servings
Preparation time – 10 minutes
Cooking time – 10 minutes
Nutritional values per serving – 198 kcals, 17 g carbs, 6 g protein, 12 g fat

Ingredients

- 4 pre-made croissants
- 100 g / 7 oz feta cheese, crumbled
- 1 tsp dried chives
- 1 tsp garlic powder
- 50 g / 3.5 oz fresh spinach, chopped

Method

1. Preheat the air fryer to 180 °C / 350 °F. Remove the mesh basket from the air fryer machine and line with parchment paper.
2. Cut the croissants in half and lay each half out on the lined mesh basket.
3. In a bowl, combine the crumbled feta cheese, dried chives, garlic powder, and chopped spinach until they form a consistent mixture.
4. Spoon some of the mixture one half of the four croissants and cover with the second half of the croissants to seal in the filling.
5. Carefully slide the croissants in the mesh basket into the air fryer machine, close the lid, and cook for 10 minutes until the pastry is crispy and the feta cheese has melted.

Simon Brookfield

Tomato and Herb Tofu

Makes 4 servings
Preparation time – 20 minutes
Cooking time – 10 minutes
Nutritional values per serving – 302 kcals, 7 g carbs, 12 g protein, 13 g fat

Ingredients

- 1 x 400 g / 14 oz block firm tofu
- 1 tbsp soy sauce
- 2 tbsp tomato paste
- 1 tsp dried oregano
- 1 tsp dried basil
- 1 tsp garlic powder

Method

1. Remove the tofu from the packaging and place on a sheet of kitchen roll. Place another sheet of kitchen roll on top of the tofu and place a plate on top of it.
2. Use something heavy to press the plate down on top of the tofu. Leave for 10 minutes to press the water out of the tofu.
3. Remove the paper towels from the tofu and chop them into even slices that are around ½ cm thick.
4. Preheat the air fryer to 180 °C / 350 °F. Remove the mesh basket from the air fryer machine and line with parchment paper.
5. Place the tofu slices on a lined baking sheet.
6. In a bowl, mix the soy sauce, tomato paste, dried oregano, dried basil, and garlic powder until fully combined.
7. Spread the mixture evenly over the tofu slices. Place the tofu slices on the baking sheet in the lined air fryer basket and cook for 10 minutes until the tofu is firm and crispy.
8. Serve the tofu slices with a side of rice or noodles and some hot vegetables.

DESSERTS AND SNACKS

Air Fryer Oatmeal and Chocolate Chip Cookies

Makes 8 servings
Preparation time – 10 minutes
Cooking time – 15 minutes
Nutritional values per serving – 112 kcals, 14 g carbs, 5 g protein, 10 g fat

Ingredients

- 4 tbsp butter, softened
- 100 g / 3.5 oz sugar
- 100 g / 3.5 oz brown sugar
- 2 eggs, beaten
- 1 tsp vanilla extract
- 400 g / 14 oz rolled oats
- 4 tbsp plain unsweetened yoghurt
- 1 tsp salt
- 200 g / 7 oz milk chocolate chips
- 2 tbsp chopped mixed nuts

Simon Brookfield

Method

1. Preheat your air fryer to 180 °C / 350 °F and line the bottom of the basket with parchment paper.
2. In a large mixing bowl, cream the butter and both sugars until they form a light and fluffy mixture.
3. Whisk in the eggs and vanilla extract until fully combined.
4. Fold in the rolled oats and stir in the yoghurt, salt, chocolate chips, and chopped mixed nuts.
5. Split the mixture into small balls and flatten into cookies. Transfer the cookies into the lined air fryer basket and close the lid.
6. Cook for 8-10 minutes until the cookies are set, golden, and crispy on the edges.
7. Once cooked, set aside to cool. Enjoy the cookies cold or reheat in the microwave and serve warm.

Air Fryer Banana Bread

Makes 4 servings
Preparation time – 10 minutes
Cooking time – 1 hour 10 minutes
Nutritional values per serving – 154 kcals, 15 g carbs, 5 g protein, 9 g fat

Ingredients

- 100 g / 3.5 oz plain flour
- 1 tsp ground cinnamon
- 1 tsp ground nutmeg
- ½ tsp baking powder
- ½ tsp salt
- 2 ripe bananas, peeled
- 2 eggs, beaten
- 100 g / 3.5 oz sugar
- 4 tbsp milk
- 2 tbsp olive oil
- 1 tsp vanilla extract
- 50 g / 3.5 oz walnuts, chopped

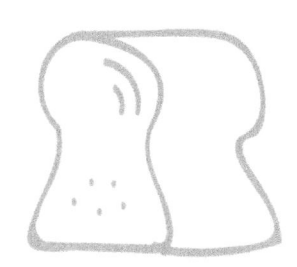

Method

1. Preheat your air fryer to 150 °C / 300 °F and line a loaf tin with parchment paper.
2. In a large mixing bowl, combine the plain flour, ground cinnamon, ground nutmeg, baking powder, and salt in a bowl.
3. Place the ripe bananas in a separate bowl and mash well. Crack the eggs into the bowl and mix well. Stir the sugar, milk, olive oil, and vanilla extract.
4. Fold the dry ingredients into the wet ingredients and mix well until fully combined.
5. Pour the batter into the prepared loaf tin and sprinkle the walnuts on top. Place the tin into the air fryer basket and cook for 30-40 minutes until set. Insert a knife into the centre of the cake. It should come out dry when the cake is fully cooked.
6. Remove the loaf tin from the air fryer and allow to cool on a wire rack before cutting into slices and serving.

Air Fryer Nutella Wedges

Makes 4 servings
Preparation time – 15 minutes
Cooking time – 10 minutes
Nutritional values per serving – 99 kcals, 12 g carbs, 3 g protein, 10 g fat

Ingredients

- 1 egg
- 1 tbsp water
- 400 g / 14 oz flaky biscuits
- 4 tbsp Nutella

Method

1. Preheat your air fryer to 150 °C / 300 °F and line the bottom of the basket with parchment paper.
2. Whisk the egg with 1 tbsp water in a small bowl.
3. Roll out the biscuits on a lightly floured clean surface. Cut the dough into 4 large wedges.
4. Lightly brush each wedge with the egg mixture.
5. Place 1 tbsp of Nutella into the centre of each biscuit wedge.
6. Fold the wedges over carefully, trying not to crack the dough. Pinch the edges of each side of the dough to seal them into small Nutella-filled pockets.
7. Place the wedges in the air fryer, close the lid, and cook for 8-10 minutes, turning over halfway through.
8. Serve the wedges while hot.

Simon Brookfield

Air Fryer Chocolate Peanut Butter Cake

Makes 4 servings
Preparation time – 10 minutes
Cooking time – 15 minutes
Nutritional values per serving – 314 kcals, 12 g carbs, 6 g protein, 9 g fat

Ingredients

- 1 tsp olive oil
- 50 g / 1.8 oz butter
- 100 g / 3.5 oz milk chocolate chips
- 4 tbsp powdered sugar
- 2 eggs, plus 2 egg yolks
- 1 tsp vanilla extract
- 4 tbsp unsweetened cocoa powder
- 100 g / 3.5 oz plain flour
- 1 tsp salt
- 4 tbsp smooth peanut butter

Method

1. Preheat your air fryer to 150 °C / 300 °F and line the bottom of the basket with parchment paper.
2. Use 1 tsp olive oil to grease 4 small circular ramekins.

3. Place the butter and chocolate chips in a heatproof bowl and cook in the microwave in 30-second intervals until fully melted.
4. Add the powdered sugar, eggs, egg yolks, and vanilla extract to the bowl, and whisk until it forms a smooth mixture. Mix in the cocoa powder, plain flour, and salt until fully combined.
5. Pour the mixture into the ramekins up to around halfway. Top each ramekin with 1 tbsp smooth peanuts butter and top with the remaining batter
6. Cover each of the ramekins with tin foil and place them into the lined air fryer basket. Cook for 10-12 minutes.
7. Remove the tin foil from the top of each ramekin and cook for a further 5 minutes.
8. Remove the ramekins from the air fryer and use a nice to run around the edges of the cakes to carefully lift them out of the ramekins.
9. Serve while hot with a sprinkle of powdered sugar or an extra dollop of peanut butter on top.

Air Fryer Puff Pastry Cherry Pies

Makes 8 servings
Preparation time – 15 minutes
Cooking time – 10 minutes
Nutritional values per serving – 298 kcals, 27 g carbs, 8 g protein, 11 g fat

Ingredients

For the puff pastry pies:

- 400 g / 14 oz cherries
- 2 tbsp stevia
- 1 tbsp corn starch
- 2 puff pastry sheets, thawed
- 1 egg

For the glaze:

- 2 tbsp heavy whipping cream
- 4 tbsp powdered sugar
- ½ tsp almond extract
- 50 g / 1.8 oz flaked almonds

The Complete XXL Air Fryer Cookbook UK

Method

1. Preheat your air fryer to 180 °C / 350 °F and line the bottom of the basket with parchment paper.
2. In a sauce pan, heat the cherries over a medium heat for 3-4 minutes until they begin to release water. Stir in 2 tbsp stevia. Lower the heat to a simmer and continue cooking for 10 minutes.
3. Meanwhile, mix the corn starch with 1 tbsp water to form a paste. Stir into the melted cherries and continue to simmer for 2 minutes until the sauce begins to thicken. Remove from the heat and set aside to cool.
4. Roll out the puff pastry dough and cut them into even squares. Spoon the cherry filling into the centre of each square of puff pastry.
5. Fold the puff pastry dough diagonally to cover the filling. Seal the edges by gently pinching them in between your thumb and fingers or using a fork.
6. Crack the egg into a bowl and whisk well. Use a pastry brush to coat the top of each pie with the egg.
7. Transfer the puff pastry cherry pies to the lined air fryer basket, close the lid, and cook for 10-12 minutes until golden brown.
8. Meanwhile, combine the heavy whipping cream, powdered sugar, and almond extract in a bowl to make the glaze.
9. Remove the puff pastry cherry pies from the air fryer and set aside to cool.
10. Once the pies have cooled, pour some of the glaze over the top of each one and top with some flaked almonds.
11. Enjoy the cherry pies hot or cold with some whipped cream on the side.

Air Fryer Chocolate Donuts

Makes 4 servings
Preparation time – 1 hour 20 minutes
Cooking time – 10 minutes
Nutritional values per serving – 355 kcals, 42 g carbs, 10 g protein, 15 g fat

Ingredients

For the donuts:

- 200 ml milk
- 100 g / 3.5 oz sugar
- 2 tsp active dry yeast (1 packet)
- 4 tbsp butter, melted
- 1 egg
- 1 tsp vanilla extract
- 400 g / 14 oz plain flour
- 4 tbsp cocoa powder

For the icing:

- 6 tbsp powdered sugar
- 2 tbsp unsweetened cocoa powder
- 100 ml heavy cream
- 50 g / 1.8 oz chopped mixed nuts

Method

1. To make the donuts, combine the milk, sugar, and yeast in a bowl. Set aside and wait for the yeast to become foamy.
2. Stir in the melted butter, egg, and vanilla extract, and mix well until the ingredients are combined.
3. Fold in the plain flour and unsweetened cocoa powder. Mix until a smooth mixture forms.

4. Lightly flour a clean surface and roll out the dough on top. Gently knead the dough for 2-3 minutes until it becomes soft and slightly tacky.
5. Transfer the dough to a large mixing bowl, cover with a clean tea towel, and leave to rise for one hour in a warm place.
6. After one hour, sprinkle some flour onto a clean surface and roll out the dough until it is around half an inch in thickness.
7. Use a round cookie cutter to create small circle donuts. Transfer the donuts to the air fryer. Don't preheat the air fryer or oil the basket.
8. Turn the air fryer onto 150 °C / 300 °F and close the lid. Cook the donuts for 8-10 minutes until set on the outside but slightly soft on the inside. Set aside while you make the icing.
9. To make the icing, combine the powdered sugar, unsweetened cocoa powder, and heavy cream in a bowl. Mix well until a smooth, sticky mixture forms.
10. Use an icing pipe or a spoon to cover the top of each donut with icing. Top each donut with a sprinkle of chopped mixed nuts.
11. Enjoy the donuts hot or cold for dessert.

Air Fryer Biscuits

Makes 8 servings
Preparation time – 15 minutes
Cooking time – 10 minutes
Nutritional values per serving – 134 kcals, 12 g carbs, 2 g protein, 8 g fat

Ingredients

- 400 g / 14 oz plain flour
- 2 tbsp baking powder
- 1 tbsp sugar
- ½ tsp salt
- 50 g / 1.8 oz butter
- 200 ml cashew milk

Method

1. Preheat your air fryer to 200 °C / 400 °F and line the bottom of the basket with parchment paper.
2. In a large mixing bowl, add the plain flour and butter. Mix well to form a crumb-like mixture.
3. Add the baking powder, sugar, and salt. Mix well before pouring in the cashew milk. Combine until all of the ingredients form into a smooth dough.
4. Roll the dough out on a lightly floured surface. Use a biscuit cutter to cut small, circular biscuits out of the dough.
5. Place the biscuits in the air fryer basket and close the lid of the machine. Cook for 10 minutes until golden and crispy.
6. Serve warm or cold.

Air Fryer Chocolate Brownies

Makes 4 servings
Preparation time – 5 minutes
Cooking time – 15 minutes
Nutritional values per serving – 189 kcals, 12 g carbs, 4 g protein, 9 g fat

Ingredients

- 100 g / 3.5 oz granulated sugar
- 8 tbsp cocoa powder
- 100 g / 3.5 oz plain flour
- ½ tsp baking powder
- ½ tsp salt
- 50 g / 1.8 oz butter, melted
- 1 egg

Method

1. Preheat your air fryer to 180 °C / 350 °F and line the bottom of the basket with parchment paper.
2. In a bowl, combine the sugar, cocoa powder, plain flour, baking powder, and salt. Mix well.
3. Stir in the melted butter and crack the egg into the bowl. Whisk well until all of the ingredients are fully combined.
4. Transfer the brownie batter into the prepared air fryer basket. Close the lid and cook for 15 minutes until set on the top but still slightly soft in the middle.
5. Remove the brownies from the air fryer and allow to cool before slicing into 4 servings.
6. Eat hot or cold with a dollop of ice cream or whipped cream.

Simon Brookfield

Air Fryer Lava Cake

Makes 4 servings
Preparation time – 5 minutes
Cooking time – 10 minutes
Nutritional values per serving – 359 kcals, 19 g carbs, 6 g protein, 15 g fat

Ingredients

- 100 g / 3.5 oz milk chocolate chips
- 5 tbsp butter, cubed
- 100 g / 3.5 oz sugar
- 2 large eggs, plus 2 egg yolks
- 1 tsp peppermint extract
- 100 g / 3.5 oz plain flour

Method

1. Preheat your air fryer to 180 °C / 350 °F and line the bottom of the basket with parchment paper.
2. Place the milk chocolate chips and butter in a large heatproof bowl and heat in the microwave in 30 second intervals until fully melted. Make sure to stir well in between intervals.
3. Fold in the sugar, eggs, egg yolks, and peppermint extract. Mix well.
4. Stir in the flour and continue mixing until the ingredients are fully combined.
5. Transfer the cake batter into the prepared air fryer basket and close the lid of the machine. Cook for 10-12 minutes until the cake is set on the outside but still soft in the centre.
6. Remove the cake from the air fryer and set aside to cool for at least 5 minutes before cutting into slices.
7. Serve hot or cold with a side of ice cream or whipped cream.

Chocolate and Berry Pop Tarts

Makes 8 servings
Preparation time – 15 minutes
Cooking time – 10 minutes
Nutritional values per serving – 255 kcals, 31 g carbs, 4 g protein, 15 g fat

Ingredients

For the filling:

- 50 g / 1.8 oz fresh raspberries
- 50 g / 1.8 oz fresh strawberries
- 100 g / 3.5 oz granulated sugar
- 1 tsp corn starch

For the pastry:

- 1 sheet puff pastry

For the frosting:

- 4 tbsp powdered sugar
- 2 tbsp maple syrup or honey
- Chocolate sprinkles

Method

1. Preheat the air fryer to 180 °C / 350 °F and line the mesh basket with parchment paper or grease it with olive oil.
2. Make the filling by combining the strawberries, raspberries, and granulated sugar in a saucepan. Place on medium heat until the mixture starts to boil. When it begins to boil, turn the temperature down to a low setting. Use a spoon to break up the berries and forms a smooth mixture.
3. Stir in the corn starch and let the mixture simmer for 1-2 minutes. Remove the saucepan from the heat and set aside to cool while you prepare the pastry.
4. Roll out the large sheet of puff pastry and cut it into 8 equal rectangles.
5. Spoon 2 tbsp of the cooled berry filling onto one side of each rectangle. Fold over the other side of each puff pastry rectangle to cover the filling. Press the sides down with a fork or using your fingers to seal the filling into the pastry.
6. Transfer the puff pastry rectangles into the lined air fryer basket. Cook for 10-12 minutes until the pastry is golden and crispy.
7. Meanwhile, make the frosting. Whisk together the powdered sugar, maple syrup or honey, and chocolate chips in a bowl until well combined.
8. Carefully spread a thin layer of frosting in the centre of each pop tart. Allow the frosting to set before serving.

White Chocolate Pudding

Makes 2 servings
Preparation time – 15 minutes
Cooking time – 15 minutes
Nutritional values per serving – 330 kcals, 31 g carbs, 12 g protein, 20 g fat

Ingredients

- 100 g / 3.5 oz white chocolate
- 50 g brown sugar
- 2 tbsp olive oil
- ½ tsp vanilla extract
- 4 egg whites, plus two egg yolks

Method

1. Preheat the air fryer to 180 °C / 350 °F and line the mesh basket with parchment paper or grease it with olive oil.
2. Place the white chocolate in a saucepan and place it over low heat until it melts, being careful not to let the chocolate burn.
3. Stir in the brown sugar, olive oil, and vanilla extract.
4. Whisk the egg whites and egg yolks in a bowl until well combined. Fold a third of the eggs into the white chocolate mixture and stir until it forms a smooth and consistent mixture. Repeat twice more with the other two-thirds of the eggs.
5. Pour the white chocolate pudding mixture evenly into two ramekins and place the ramekins in the lined air fryer basket. Cook for 15 minutes until the pudding is hot and set on top.

Milk and White Chocolate Chip Air Fryer Donuts with Frosting

Makes 4 servings
Preparation time – 1 hour 20 minutes
Cooking time – 10 minutes
Nutritional values per serving – 412 kcals, 44 g carbs, 11 g protein, 17 g fat

Ingredients

For the donuts:

- 200 ml milk (any kind)
- 50 g / 3.5 oz brown sugar
- 50 g / 3.5 oz granulated sugar
- 1 tbsp active dry yeast
- 2 tbsp olive oil
- 4 tbsp butter, melted
- 1 egg, beaten
- 1 tsp vanilla extract
- 400 g / 14 oz plain flour
- 4 tbsp cocoa powder
- 100 g / 3.5 oz milk chocolate chips

For the frosting:

- 5 tbsp powdered sugar
- 2 tbsp cocoa powder
- 100 ml heavy cream
- 50 g / 1.8 oz white chocolate chips, melted

Method

1. To make the donuts, whisk together the milk, brown and granulated sugars, and active dry yeast in a bowl. Set aside for a few minutes while the yeast starts to get foamy.

2. Stir the melted butter, beaten egg, and vanilla extract into the bowl. Mix well until all of the ingredients are combined.

3. Fold in the plain flour and cocoa powder until a smooth mixture forms.

4. Lightly flour a clean kitchen top surface and roll the dough out. Gently knead the dough for 2-3 minutes until it becomes soft and slightly tacky.

5. Transfer the dough into a large mixing bowl and cover it with a clean tea towel or some tinfoil. Leave the dough to rise for around one hour in a warm place.

6. Remove the tea towel or tinfoil from the bowl and roll it out on a floured surface once again. Use a rolling pin to roll the dough into a one-inch thick circle.

7. Use a round cookie cutter to create circular donuts and place each one into a lined air fryer basket.

8. Once all of the donuts have been placed into the air fryer, turn the machine onto 150 °C / 300 °F and close the lid.

9. Cook the donuts for 8-10 minutes until they are slightly golden and crispy on the outside.

10. While the donuts are cooking in the air fryer, make the frosting by combining the powdered sugar, cocoa powder, heavy cream, and melted white chocolate chips in a bowl. Mix well until a smooth, sticky mixture forms.

11. When the donuts are cooked, remove them from the air fryer and set aside to cool for 5-10 minutes. Once cooled, evenly spread some frosting on the top layer of each one. Place in the fridge to set for at least one hour.

12. Enjoy the donuts hot or cold.

Coffee, Chocolate Chip, and Banana Bread

Makes 8 servings
Preparation time – 10 minutes
Cooking time – 1 hour 10 minutes
Nutritional values per serving – 189 kcals, 17 g carbs, 10 g protein, 10 g fat

Ingredients

- 200 g / 7 oz plain flour
- 1 tsp baking powder
- 1 tsp ground cinnamon
- 1 tbsp ground coffee
- ½ tsp salt
- 2 ripe bananas, peeled
- 2 eggs, beaten
- 100 g / 3.5 oz granulated sugar
- 50 g / 3.5 oz brown sugar
- 100 g / 3.5 oz milk chocolate chips
- 4 tbsp milk
- 2 tbsp olive oil
- 1 tsp vanilla extract

Method

1. Preheat the air fryer to 150 °C / 300 °F and line a loaf tin with parchment paper.
2. In a large mixing bowl, combine the plain flour, baking powder, ground cinnamon, and salt.
3. Mash the ripe bananas in a separate bowl until there are no lumps. Whisk in the beaten eggs, followed by the granulated sugar, brown sugar, and milk chocolate chips until well combined.
4. Stir in the milk, olive oil, and vanilla extract before combining the dry and wet ingredients. Mix until combined into one smooth mixture.
5. Pour the batter into the prepared loaf tin and transfer into the air fryer basket. Cook for 30-40 minutes until the cake is set and golden on top. Insert a knife into the centre of the cake. It should come out dry when the cake is fully cooked.
6. Remove the loaf tin from the air fryer and set aside to cool on a drying rack. Once cooled, remove the cake from the loaf tin and cut into slices.
7. Enjoy the cake hot or cold.

White Chocolate and Raspberry Loaf

Makes 8 servings
Preparation time – 10 minutes
Cooking time – 1 hour 10 minutes
Nutritional values per serving – 189 kcals, 17 g carbs, 10 g protein, 10 g fat

Ingredients

- 400 g / 14 oz plain flour
- 2 tsp baking powder
- 1 tsp ground cinnamon
- ½ tsp salt
- 3 eggs, beaten
- 50 g / 3.5 oz granulated sugar
- 50 g / 3.5 oz brown sugar
- 100 g / 3.5 oz white chocolate chips
- 100 g / 3.5 oz fresh raspberries
- 1 tbsp cocoa powder
- 4 tbsp milk
- 1 tsp vanilla extract

Method

1. Preheat the air fryer to 150 °C / 300 °F and line a loaf tin with parchment paper.
2. Combine the plain flour, baking powder, ground cinnamon, and salt in a large mixing bowl.
3. Whisk eggs into the bowl, then stir in the granulated sugar and brown sugar. Mix well before folding in the white chocolate chips, fresh raspberries, cocoa powder, milk, and vanilla extract.
4. Stir the mixture until it is lump-free and transfer into a lined loaf tin. Place the loaf tin into the lined air fryer basket, close the lid, and cook for 30-40 minutes.
5. The cake should be golden and set by the end of the cooking process. Insert a knife into the centre of the cake. It should come out dry when the cake is fully cooked.
6. Remove the cake from the air fryer, still in the loaf tin. Set aside to cool on a drying rack for 20-30 minutes before cutting into slices and serving.

Chocolate-Glazed Banana Slices

Makes 2 servings
Preparation time – 10 minutes
Cooking time – 10 minutes
Nutritional values per serving – 200 kcals, 5 g carbs, 6 g protein, 8 g fat

Ingredients

- 2 bananas
- 1 tbsp honey
- 1 tbsp chocolate spread, melted
- 2 tbsp milk chocolate chips

Method

1. Preheat the air fryer to 180 °C / 350 °F. Remove the mesh basket from the machine and line it with parchment paper.
2. Cut the two bananas into even slices and place them in the lined air fryer basket.
3. In a small bowl, mix the honey and melted chocolate spread. Use a brush to glaze the banana slices. Carefully press the milk chocolate chips into the banana slices enough so that they won't fall out when you transfer the bananas into the air fryer.
4. Carefully slide the mesh basket into the air fryer, close the lid, and cook for 10 minutes until the bananas are hot and the choc chips have melted.
5. Enjoy the banana slices on their own or with a side of ice cream.

Chocolate Souffle

Makes 2 servings
Preparation time – 10 minutes
Cooking time – 15 minutes
Nutritional values per serving – 401 kcals, 29 g carbs, 10 g protein, 13 g fat

Ingredients

- 2 eggs
- 4 tbsp brown sugar
- 1 tsp vanilla extract
- 4 tbsp butter, melted
- 4 tbsp milk chocolate chips
- 4 tbsp flour

Method

1. Preheat the air fryer to 180 °C / 350 °F. Remove the mesh basket from the machine and line it with parchment paper.
2. Separate the egg whites from the egg yolks and place them in two separate bowls.
3. Beat the yolks together with the brown sugar, vanilla extract, melted butter, milk chocolate chips, and flour in a bowl. It should form a smooth, consistent mixture.
4. Whisk the egg whites until they form stiff peaks. In batches, fold the egg whites into the chocolate mixture.
5. Divide the batter evenly between two souffle dishes and place them in the lined air fryer basket.
6. Cook the souffle dishes for 15 minutes until hot and set.

Apple and Cinnamon Puff Pastry Pies

Makes 8 servings
Preparation time – 15 minutes
Cooking time – 20 minutes
Nutritional values per serving – 301 kcals, 40 g carbs, 9 g protein, 13 g fat

Ingredients

- 4 tbsp butter
- 4 tbsp white sugar
- 2 tbsp brown sugar
- 1 tsp cinnamon
- 1 tsp nutmeg
- 1 tsp salt
- 4 apples, peeled and diced
- 2 large sheets puff pastry
- 1 egg

Method

1. Preheat the air fryer to 180 °C / 350 °F. Remove the mesh basket from the machine and line it with parchment paper.
2. In a bowl, whisk together the butter, white sugar, brown sugar, cinnamon, nutmeg, and salt.
3. Place the apples in a heatproof baking dish and coat them in the butter and sugar mixture. Transfer to the air fryer and cook for 10 minutes.
4. Meanwhile, roll out the pastry on a clean, floured surface. Cut the sheets into 8 equal parts.
5. Once the apples are hot and softened, evenly spread the mixture between the pastry sheets. Fold the sheets over to cover the apple and gently press the edges using a fork or your fingers to seal the mixture in.
6. Beat the egg in a bowl and use a brush to coat the top of each pastry sheet.
7. Carefully transfer the filled pastry sheets to the prepared air fryer basket, close the lid, and cook for 10 minutes until the pastry is golden and crispy.

EXCLUSIVE BONUS

40 Weight Loss Recipes

&

14 Days Meal Plan

Scan the QR-Code and receive the FREE download:

Disclaimer

This book contains opinions and ideas of the author and is meant to teach the reader informative and helpful knowledge while due care should be taken by the user in the application of the information provided. The instructions and strategies are possibly not right for every reader and there is no guarantee that they work for everyone. Using this book and implementing the information/recipes therein contained is explicitly your own responsibility and risk. This work with all its contents, does not guarantee correctness, completion, quality or correctness of the provided information. Misinformation or misprints cannot be completely eliminated.

Printed in Great Britain
by Amazon